"Few have been able to combine apolo[illegible] evangelism into one practical volume for equipping the church. Steven Garofalo's book does just that. I highly recommend *Equipped* for your edification and understanding so you can be genuinely prepared to defend and advance the Christian faith."

Josh McDowell
Founder, Josh McDowell Ministry
Author of *The New Evidence That Demands a Verdict* and 40 other books

"This book is clear, correct, and concise. I am happy to recommend it. Everyone who desires to defend the faith needs to read this excellent work."

Dr. Norman L. Geisler
Author of over 100 books, Speaker, and Distinguished Professor at Southern Evangelical Seminary and Veritas International University

"Steven Garofalo has distilled a mountain of biblical and theological information into one small practical volume to help all of us communicate the gospel with love and truth to our contemporary culture. He skillfully deals with such common questions as "Is Jesus the only way?" and "If God is good, what about all of the evil?" Buy *Equipped* and share it with others."

Dr. John Munro
Senior Pastor, Calvary Church, Charlotte, NC

"As one who has been involved in ministry for over twenty years, it is part of the calling for a pastor/teacher to equip the local church for the work of the ministry (Ephesians 4:11–12). In *Equipped*, Steven Garofalo provides a tool to help make that job a lot easier. As Steven says, 'Being equipped is not optional.'"

Jeremy R. Varner
Senior Pastor, Community Baptist Church, La Grange, NC

"Our youth are ill equipped by our churches for the coming potential spiritual and intellectual avalanches they'll face when entering the university. Parents and grandparents ought to be concerned. All people ought to be concerned in this rapidly secularizing culture. Reading *Equipped* will enable you to help a fellow believer or an unbeliever have confidence in God. Informative and understandable, this book winsomely covers the various worldviews and several comparative religions. It also gives reasons to believe and effective ways to share your Christian faith."

Dr. Corey Miller

President/CEO of Ratio Christi, Adjunct professor of Comparative Religions and Philosophy at Indiana University, Author of Leaving Mormonism: Why Four Scholars Changed Their Minds

"*Equipped* answers some of the basic questions asked about Christianity and religion, then presents a practical plan to help Christians present the truth of God by using apologetics in evangelism. Steven Garofalo has developed an excellent tool for Christians to defend and advance the Christian faith in the twenty-first century. I highly recommend this book."

Kent Suter

Youth Pastor, Cornerstone Bible College, Lilburn, GA

EQUIPPED

Basic Training in Apologetics for Evangelism

STEVEN GAROFALO

Charlotte, NC

Equipped: Basic Training in Apologetics for Evangelism
Copyright ©2018 Steven Garofalo
Published by TriedStone Publishing Company
P.O. Box 79148
Charlotte, NC 28271
www.TriedStonePublishing.com

All rights reserved solely by the author. No part of this publication may be reproduced, stored in a retrieval system, or transmitted in any form by any means—electronic, mechanical, photocopy, recording, or otherwise—without the prior permission of the publisher, except as provided by USA copyright law.

Editor: Denise Loock

Cover design: Steve Mast

First printing 2018

Printed in the United States of America

All Scripture quotations, unless otherwise indicated, are taken from *The Holy Bible: New International Version.*® Copyright © 1973, 1978, 1984, 1986, 2011 by Biblica, Inc.™ Used by permission of Zondervan. All rights reserved worldwide. www.zondervan.com. The "NIV" and "New International Version" are trademarks registered in the United States Patent and Trademark office by Biblica, Inc.™

Scripture quotations marked NASB are taken from *The New American Standard Bible*® Copyright © 1960, 1962, 1963, 1968, 1971, 1972, 1973, 1975, 1977, 1995 by The Lockman Foundation. Used by permission.

Scripture quotations marked ESV are taken from *The Holy Bible, English Standard Version* ® (ESV ®), copyright © 2001, by Crossway, a publishing ministry of Good News Publishers. Used by permission. All rights reserved.

Library of Congress Cataloging-in-Publication Data
Library of Congress Control Number 2018908820
Garofalo, Steven
Equipped: Basic Training in Christian Apologetics for Evangelism / Steven Garofalo

ISBN 978-0-9897446-4-5 (TPB: Alk. Paper)

. 1. Apologetics. 1. Garofalo, Steven. (Steven Garofalo),
LLCN 2018908820

To my son, Zacharia, and my precious daughters, Arabel and Amelia.
May you own your faith and know why you believe what you believe.
May you continue to learn and be equipped to defend the Christian faith
in a world that is often against the things of God.
May you always share that faith in truth and love with others.
God has provided each of you with special gifts
and a calling according to his will for your lives.
I pray that I have been able to equip you in all areas,
especially with the ability to defend and advance your faith in Jesus Christ.
I love you all immeasurably. Daddy.

To my godly wife, Heather,
who is in the trenches, equipping our children on a daily basis.
A lot of the equipping in our household can be attributed to you.
I love you more than words can express,
and I am thankful that the Lord has provided me with you—
a godly wife and mother to our children.
I am blessed with a wonderful family
in the present and forever more into eternity.

EQUIPPED

And he gave the apostles, the prophets, the evangelists, the shepherds and teachers, to equip the saints for the work of ministry, for building up the body of Christ, until we all attain to the unity of the faith and of the knowledge of the Son of God, to mature manhood, to the measure of the stature of the fullness of Christ, so that we may no longer be children, tossed to and fro by the waves and carried about by every wind of doctrine, by human cunning, by craftiness in deceitful schemes. Rather, speaking the truth in love, we are to grow up in every way into him who is the head, into Christ, from whom the whole body, joined and held together by every joint with which it is equipped, when each part is working properly, makes the body grow so that it builds itself up in love. Ephesians 4:11–16 (ESV)

CONTENTS

FOREWORD

Apologetics is the art of defending the truth of Christianity from its many attacks. But there exists today a gap between the study of apologetics and its use in personal evangelism. By answering six of the most important questions related to using apologetics and evangelism, Steven Garofalo has done something unique in equipping today's Christian. The author gives us helpful insights into some difficult scenarios and answers some of the most challenging questions asked about God and Christianity.

Steven's many years of apologetics study (including a Master of Arts degree in Apologetics), teaching, and personal evangelism qualify him to pursue what lies *behind* the objections to Christianity and answer *those* objections as well as what is on the surface. The author unveils the false assumptions made against Christianity and shows how this is useful in evangelism. Rather than simply presenting abstract arguments, Steven's personal experience provides real-life stories alongside important information, helping the average reader become well-versed in apologetics on a practical level. It is evident in these stories that he is not obnoxious or rude in defending the Christian faith. Instead, he uses tactics and strategies that help others see the weakness of their objections with the goal of winning them to Christ. This is what makes this book unique.

Many today think that every religion leads to the same place.

Equipped addresses this issue (religious pluralism), and in doing so helps readers understand their own worldview. The author addresses questions about the existence of God, moral absolutes, and why God allows pain and suffering. These are some of the greatest objections to the Christian faith. Also, since the question of morality impacts nearly all other questions relating to God, religion, and Christianity, he is careful to address the issue of morality as a separate chapter. His conclusion is that only the God of the Bible can be the Ultimate Authority regarding moral absolutes.

Few have been able to combine apologetics and evangelism into one practical volume for equipping the church. Steven Garofalo's book does just that. I highly recommend *Equipped* to you for your edification and understanding so you can be genuinely prepared to defend and advance the Christian faith.

Josh McDowell
August 2018

ACKNOWLEDGMENTS

I would like to acknowledge my mom, Vita Delores Garofalo. My dad Mauro passed away suddenly in 1970, leaving my mom to raise four children on her own. My sister was only a week old, I had just turned five years of age, and my brothers were nine and eleven. Three short years later, Mom was diagnosed with leukemia and given six months to live. She survived and was determined to make certain that, in case she relapsed, her children would be equipped to not only survive but also thrive in a very difficult world.

Mom often spoke to me and my siblings in life-lesson parables, just as her mom, my grandma, did. Mom's parables were more often than not tied to the parables and moral lessons found in Scripture. She also repeated, with seriousness and intentionality, three important principles. First, she reminded us that what lies ahead is always subject to "God willing." Second, she always gave credit to "the hand of God" for making it possible for us to stay together as a family and encouraged us to do the same. Third, Mom always told my siblings and me that, despite our differences, we should keep in touch with one another and consistently tell one another "I love you." Those principles formed the backbone of our family.

My mom raised us children on an administrative assistant's salary. She deserves a PhD for her determination, wisdom, and accounting skills.

She used envelopes to manage her finances, and nobody, including her children, can figure out how she did it. The only explanation is the hand of God. She and my father were determined that all their children would go to college and be equipped with an undergraduate degree. All of us met that goal. More importantly, Mom helped to equip us with life skills and faith in God so we could thrive in a tough world.

Mom, thank you for the gift of being equipped with a reverence for God and a determination to live by biblical principles—a gift that has carried me through many difficult challenges and into a deep relationship with God. I love you, Mom.

In Memory of Mauro Garofalo (September 20, 1928–June 19, 1970)

I also want to acknowledge a few other folks who have contributed to this manuscript. Dr. John Munro, senior pastor of Calvary Church in Charlotte, NC, has had an immeasurable impact on our whole family. You equip my wife and me weekly. My older daughter takes notes on Sunday morning. My younger daughter and my son listen intently to his sermons, and my son recites the basic points when we get home. We are blessed and appreciative that God provided such a godly man as our pastor during a period of history when the truth of God's Word is not always preached from America's pulpits. Thanks also to our church family at Calvary for supporting us in so many ways.

Dr. Norman Geisler, you have also had a tremendous impact on our family. After twenty years as my personal advisor, everybody in the Garofalo family loves you and your wife Barbara. We appreciate all that you have given our family in terms of Dr. Geisler's writings, our friendship, being our neighbor, and the powerful example and role model you have set in your sixty-plus years of marriage. This book would not have been written without you.

Josh McDowell, you also played a major role in this book as well as in my early spiritual growth. *More Than a Carpenter* was one of the first books I read as a new Christian. You have shown me how to be both an apologist and an evangelist.

Acknowledgements

Pastor Kent Suter, you have dedicated your life to God, students, and others. Thank you, Kent, for your friendship, wisdom, and much more.

I am also grateful for my editor, Denise Loock, who took the time and energy to edit this project with the highest literary and biblical standards. Thanks to Steve Mast, my book cover designer. Your creative giftedness is the first thing folks see, and God will use it to advance the message of this manuscript.

Finally, thanks to Southern Evangelical Seminary (SES). The faculty and staff at SES have helped to mold and equip me to complete my ministry calling. I am grateful for all my professors and the administrative staff that keep SES vibrantly moving forward.

INTRODUCTION

If you give me ten minutes to chop down a tree, I'll spend my first two minutes sharpening my ax.[1] —C. S. Lewis

On Monday, December 11, 2006, the world awoke to the news of three men, all in their thirties, who had gone missing on Mt. Hood in Oregon. The three experienced climbers set out to climb the 11,239-foot mountain via a route on the perilous north face in the most difficult time to climb—winter. Two of the three climbers were highly experienced. One had climbed Mt. Hood fourteen times. Despite their level of experience and their superb professional gear, they were not equipped for what lay ahead of them. As a result, all three perished on Mount Hood. One of the men—Kelly James of Dallas, Texas—stayed in a snow cave the three climbers built while the other two climbers went for help. James used his cell phone to contact his wife. He told her that he was not doing well and that he loved her and their family. That was the last message anyone received from the climbers.

On December 18, 2006, rescuers found the snow cave. James had frozen to death. His waterlogged cell phone lay alongside his body. Cause of death? Hypothermia. At the cave, rescuers also found climbing equipment—including two slings and two aluminum anchors driven into the snow—which led rescuers to believe that James's companions, Brian Hall and Jerry "Nikko" Cooke, had tried to secure themselves to the steep slope. That was the last sign of them.

A snowstorm had rolled in while the men were on the mountain. According to an article in *The New York Times*, the Hood River County sheriff said that "the climbers may have fallen in a steep section known as 'the gullies' near Eliot Glacier, and that they could have encountered an avalanche. The climbers had begun their ascent on December 8, planning to reach the top, then descend in a single day. They made it to the top, but they did not survive the descent.

Photographs on James's camera showed that the climbers were "lightly equipped but well equipped," according to the sheriff. After looking at the equipment in the photographs, the sheriff said he was "pretty concerned" about how long somebody could last out there.[2] In the climbers' vehicle, officials also found a note, which listed the equipment the men planned to take and a brief description of the mountains they had climbed. You see, despite the fact that the three men had the best gear, they did not use it. Instead, they packed lightly for what they expected would be a relatively short though difficult traverse up Mount Hood. What they failed to do was pack as they should, which would have entailed the proper gear and supplies for a prolonged trip in case of a snowstorm, avalanche, or other unforeseen event.

Being fully equipped with the proper gear is essential.

The tragic story of the Mt. Hood climbers is a good analogy for today's church, which often equips its students with little, if any, plan for the spiritual avalanches and snowstorms guaranteed to come their way—at the university and beyond. The result, in part, is that between 70–75 percent of Christian youth leave the church after high school.[3]

These American young people are not being equipped to defend or advance their faith, despite the skeptical and atheistic views they encounter in the world and at the university after they leave home. On average, college professors are five times more likely to identify themselves as atheists than the general public.[4] Too many Christian students are not equipped to resist the overwhelmingly liberal academic agenda of professors who are set on destroying their faith and converting them to atheism.

When young people leave home for the first time, often to become college students, they are attracted by all the secular world offers through friendship, sex, drugs, alcohol, and misguided causes. As a result, they check their faith at the door of their college classrooms because they are challenged with questions that many churches are unable or unwilling to address. Other churches simply have not made the effort to properly equip their students.

Church programs such as AWANA teach kids to memorize large amounts of Scripture. But the ability to recite Scripture is an inadequate weapon by itself. Young people need to be able to apply Scripture; therefore, apologetics training is no longer a luxury. It is an essential part of equipping today's youth and adults to defend and advance their Christian faith. Whether you live in the northern United States, the southern United States, or anywhere else in the world, the agenda of secular evangelists and apologists as well the challenges of their worldviews are real. The assault on Christian values and on our Christian youth is no longer limited to one segment of culture or geography. There is no place on the face of the planet that is safe from a world ready to challenge the Christian worldview.

According to an article in *The Oregonian*, an estimated 10,000 people a year attempt to climb Mount Hood. "Every year, 20–25 of them have to be rescued with the help of rescue sleds or by helicopter."[5] I wish I could say that we only have to rescue 20–25 Christian young people from secular deprogramming, but sadly, the number is exponentially higher than that of annual Mount Hood rescues: closer to 7,000 out of every 10,000.

We can blame much of this on ourselves—that is, on the church. While there are exceptions, most American churches overemphasize emotional experience and ignore biblical commands to develop the mind (1 Peter 3:15; 2 Corinthians 10:5). Years ago, we, the church, started to study the Bible and to discipline and equip our students to stand on their own faith. When Christian conversion rates began to drop in the late 1970s and the early 1980s, the church flipped from studying the Bible and discipleship with the reward of social activities and entertainment to focusing on social activities and entertainment with Bible study (developing the mind) as a secondary focus. As a result, students in the twenty-first century believe that they have to feel what is truth and what is true about God instead of what they know to be factual evidence about the true God and religion.

The apostle Paul, who wrote almost half of the Bible's New Testament, preached the gospel throughout the Roman Empire. The book of Acts says this about his methods: *But Paul increased all the more in strength, and confounded the Jews who lived in Damascus by proving that Jesus was the Christ* (Acts 9:22 ESV). The word *prove,* as defined by Webster's Dictionary, means "to establish the existence, truth, or validity of" (as by evidence or logic).[6] Notice that Paul proved the fact that Jesus Christ is the Christ though the mind. Paul lived in an expressive culture where passion and emotion were part of the culture. Therefore, he did not ignore the passionate plea of and to the heart; instead, he led with the head and appealed to the heart. We should do the same. Jesus commanded us to apply our minds to truth when he said to *"love the Lord your God with all your heart and with all your soul and with all your* ***mind****"* (Matthew 22:37, emphasis added).

With as many as 83 percent of Christian students abandoning their faith during the first year of college—most within the first thirty days—we must admit that our students are ill-equipped for the secular world. Through the prophet Isaiah, God tells us, *"I equip you, though you do not know me, that people may know, from the rising of the sun and from the west, that there is none beside me"* (Isaiah 45:5 ESV). The New International Version says it this way: *"I will strengthen you, though you have not acknowledged me."*

The mission of this book is threefold. First, inoculate our youth for the secular world they are about to enter. Second, shore up and strengthen the faith of all believers who have been called by God to live out their faith in God through Jesus Christ in a highly secular New Age culture. Third, equip students, young adults, parents, and grandparents with a basic training in Christian apologetics. Why? We must be better able to defend the Christian faith and better equipped to execute the Great Commission (Matthew 28) through sharing our faith.

In February 2018, popular television host Joy Behar responded to Vice President Mike Pence's statement of Christian faith by saying, "It's one thing to talk to Jesus; it's another thing when Jesus talks to you. That's called mental illness, if I'm not correct."[7] Ms. Behar influences millions of people worldwide with her anti-Christian views. What are we doing to equip ourselves and the younger generations to stand strong as well as share their faith with people such as Ms. Behar? We no longer can rely on the Four Spiritual Laws alone when defending and sharing our faith. We must add keen, well-constructed apologetics to our evangelism efforts.

The Mount Hood climbers thought they could conquer one of the highest, most dangerous mountains in America in the dead of winter with light gear. They were wrong. They all had professional gear, but they were not fully equipped—even though they assumed they were.

We can avoid their error. We must not think that we, or the younger generations, are well equipped in our Christian faith simply because we, or they, grew up in the church. One of the three Oregon climbers made a similar assumption—after all, he had climbed Mt. Hood fourteen times. But despite their high level of experience, the climbers were not equipped for the worst conditions. The same can be said for most of us.

My prayer is that *Equipped* will help you sharpen your ax so that when you undertake the task of living and sharing your Christian faith, you will be biblically and apologetically equipped for the God-ordained task at hand. Please take notes, learn the information, and enjoy the journey.

Worldview = mental model of reality, framework of ideas about the world

Three Main World Views
① Theism - God made all ② Atheism - No God ③ Pantheism - God is all
Judaism, Christianity, Islam   Buddhism, Taoism   Zen Buddhism, Hindu, New Age
Five minor world views
Life transformation happens when you believe absolute truth.

CHAPTER 1

EVERYONE HAS A WORLDVIEW: WHAT'S YOURS?

A person's worldview ... reflects how he would answer all the "big questions" of human existence: fundamental questions about who and what we are, where we came from, why we're here, where (if anywhere) we're headed, the meaning and purpose of life, the nature of the afterlife, and what counts as a good life here and now.[1] —James Anderson / Ligonier Ministries

Early in December of 2015, one week after the San Bernardino, California, terrorist attack that killed fourteen people and injured twenty-two, my cell phone rang. My wife was calling me from outside our house. I was inside, in our home office. Her voice was laced with concern as she told me the home-contractor company representative had arrived as scheduled. His name was Muhammad, and he had a large

Bowie knife. As I calmly went outside to meet Muhammad, I asked myself, "Shouldn't I give this person who looks like a Muslim, has the name Muhammad, and is carrying a large Bowie knife a reason for the truth and hope that we as Christians have?" (1 Peter 3:15).

I wondered how Muhammad viewed the world. As a Muslim, he probably subscribed to the theory of absolute truth. Metaphysical Relativism proclaims there are no absolutes anywhere in reality, and Epistemological Relativism proclaims there are no absolutes in human knowledge—that knowledge in relation to truth is relative to things such as time, space, culture, society, and history. I surmised that Muhammad didn't embrace any category of relativism because, while the Islamic faith is wrong about who God is, it is right about moral absolutes and absolute truth. So my starting point for sharing Christ with someone like Muhammad is to reason from absolute truth that a theistic God of the universe exists. Then I make my way to the fact that Jesus Christ *is* Truth. If Muhammad were an atheist or agnostic, I'd start by addressing the belief that truth is relative, which would render the existence of God and the person of Jesus Christ as the true God relative. I decided to approach Muhammad by addressing what truth *is*.

First, *truth is what corresponds to reality.* This includes the fact that truth is transcultural. By this I mean that 2 + 2 = 4 in all cultures for all people at all times. Born in America, I am the son of a Sicilian immigrant, and I was raised in Western culture according to the Christian faith and absolute truth. From his accent, I deduced Muhammad had probably been born in India, where the philosophical and theological position about truth is relative. However, as a Muslim, Muhammad would surely reject relativism. I saw this potential conflict as a good starting point for sharing the Truth of Jesus Christ with him. If I could get Muhammad to reason for truth, then I could show him logically that just as 2 + 2 = 4 for Muslims, Hindus, and Christians, it is also true that as the Son of God, Jesus Christ *is* God and not just a prophet. This would create a starting point for me to share the truth that Jesus is the true God.

Second, *truth is telling it as it really is.* In John 18:38, Pilate asked Jesus, "*What is truth?*" This indicates that Pilate knew some truth. Furthermore, by telling the screaming mob that he could find no fault in Jesus, Pilate was telling it like it is. In our politically correct world, telling it like it really is has become intolerance—in the name of tolerance.[2] The truth is that political correctness is hypocritical, self-defeating, and unable to withstand the truth. Truth levels the playing field in that God asks us to use fair and balanced scales: *Honest scales and balances belong to the Lord; all the weights in the bag are of his making* (Proverbs 16:11). Furthermore, *The Lord detests differing weights, and dishonest scales do not please him* (Proverbs 20:23). While the verse refers to the weighing of metals as currency, the principle it speaks to is honesty in all of life's transactions—including how we use words. Political correctness is man's effort to control the meaning of words and truth; therefore, political correctness is at odds with truth because *telling it as it is* means speaking the truth, including the truth about God.

Truth is what is. The earth is round, not flat. Jesus Christ is the Son of God, not just a prophet, or a great religious, moral man. The First Principles of Logic—the simple logical essentials behind the process by which we discover all things about and in the world—affirms this.[3] One of the First Principles, the Law of Noncontradiction, says that opposite ideas cannot be true and not true at the same time and in the same sense. This means that Islam and Christianity cannot both be truth at the same time and in the same sense. The same can be said of Christianity and Hinduism, which simply means, "the religion of India."[4] The medieval Muslim philosopher Avicenna said, "Anyone who denies the Law of Noncontradiction should be beaten and burned until he admits that to be beaten is not the same as to not be beaten, and to be burned is not the same as to not be burned!"[5]

The First Principles of Logic tell it like it is. These principles are tools we use to discover all other truths. Without them, we could not learn anything else. By not telling the truth, or not saying it like it is, we become confused about knowing anything absolutely. This seemed like a good starting point for my conversation with Muhammad.

In giving a reason for truth, I could proclaim that truth can be known, which, in turn, leads to the conclusion that the truth about God can be known. If truth can be known, then we can absolutely know which god is the true God. By exposing the truth about the absolute truth, we clear the way to the absolute existence of the true God of the universe.

While I was greeting Muhammad, my mobile phone rang. A friend had called to encourage me and to let me know that he was praying for my ministry. I thanked him for praying for us, and I made sure Muhammad heard the conversation as a precursor to asking him about his cultural and religious beliefs.

As Muhammad and I got to know each other, I found out he carried the Bowie knife because he ran into snakes and varmints when he worked under residential crawl spaces. He confirmed that he was indeed from India and that he and his family had grown up in the Islamic faith. But after they had come to America, he, his mother, and his two brothers had all accepted Jesus Christ as Savior. In fact, they attended a local church pastored by a dear friend of mine who ministers to a multicultural community.

I no longer had doubts about Muhammad's worldview. As we talked, I saw the love of God—of Jesus Christ—in him. Walking back inside my home, I realized that we never know whom we are speaking with. I was thankful Muhammad was a believer in Jesus Christ, but I was reminded again how we must always be ready and willing to give a reason for the truth and the hope that lies within us as believers in Jesus Christ, even when it seems uncomfortable or politically incorrect.

WHAT IS A WORLDVIEW?

A worldview is a mental model of reality—a framework of ideas and attitudes about the world, ourselves, and life; a comprehensive system of beliefs with answers to a wide range of life's questions such as these: what are humans, why are we here, and what is our purpose?[6] All worldviews lead back to questions about God:

- Can we know God exists?
- Have miracles occurred in the past as the Bible claims, and do they occur in the present?
- Does God communicate with us, and if so, how?
- What happens to us after death?

Theologian and Philosopher Dr. Norman Geisler defines worldview as "an interpretive framework through which or by which we make sense out of the data of life. It is how we view or interpret reality. If God and the universe exist, then either there is one God or many gods. If there are many gods, then the polytheistic worldview is correct. If there is only one God, then this God is either finite or infinite. If there is one finite god, then finite *godism* is correct. If this finite god has two poles, one being beyond and one in the world, then *pantheism* (god is in all) is right. If there is one infinite God—as Judaism, Christianity, and Islam assert—then God either intervenes in the world and the universe, or he does not. If there is intervention, then *theism* (God created all) is true. If God does not intervene in the world and universe, then *deism* (God created all but does not intervene) is true."[7]

Through our worldview, we determine our priorities, our relationship with God, and our relationship with our fellow human beings. Our worldview instructs and directs our entire life, answering questions like a road map that provides direction and guidance. Understanding worldviews, therefore, is essential to perceiving how other people understand the world around them, the universe, and most important, how they understand God.

EVERYONE HAS A WORLDVIEW

A worldview is like a set of glasses that clarifies or taints our vision of God, objectivity, and morality. Our worldview is formed through our educational experience, our family upbringing, our culture, the books we read, and the influence of the media we subscribe to. Most of us have never given great thought to what we believe. In many cases, we may be unable to state a rational defense for our beliefs. The Christian worldview is theistic. Christians believe that God exists (Hebrews 11:6) and that God, not man, is the measure of all things. God created everything that exists, including us (Genesis 1:1), and Jesus holds everything together (Colossians 1:17).

Theologian A. W. Tozer made this observation: "Were we able to extract from any man a complete answer to the question, 'What comes into your mind when you think about God?' we might predict with certainty the spiritual future of that man."[8] Tozer was saying, in part, that every individual's understanding of the nature of God ultimately affects their worldview, which, in turn, determines what they believe about morality and how they live out that morality. Each worldview defines God differently and holds to a view that is equally exclusive and narrow. Each worldview is incompatible with all the other worldviews because of its differing claims about God.

An examination of the evidence leads to this question: "What makes a non-Christian worldview deceptive?" A deceptive worldview is one in which Satan tries to con us into thinking a certain set of beliefs is absolute truth, when in reality it is not. While it looks like the truth on the surface, it is laced with lies.

THE THREE MAJOR WORLDVIEWS

Scripture warns us to not be taken captive by the deceptive philosophies and worldviews spreading throughout our culture (Colossians 2:8). In this section, we will define and evaluate the three major worldviews—pantheism, atheism, and theism—and show why they cannot all be true.

- **PANTHEISM: GOD IS ALL** (includes Zen Buddhism, Hinduism, and New Age)
- **ATHEISM: NO GOD AT ALL** (includes Buddhism, Taoism, and Religious Humanism)
- **THEISM: GOD MADE ALL** (includes Judaism, Christianity, and Islam)

Judaism, Christianity, and Islam are the three major world religions. They all fall under the theistic worldview. The other two major worldviews are non-theistic. They are no longer found only in faraway countries; they are prevalent in communities, doctor's offices, gas stations, and office cubicles all across the United States.

Atheism and theism are mutually exclusive worldviews. Because each holds to certain narrow beliefs, it is logically impossible to also hold a contrasting worldview. To make such a claim would be self-contradicting and, in turn, self-defeating.[9] For example, while atheism holds to the belief that there is no God at all, theism holds to only one, supernatural God. These two views are obviously incompatible because they contradict one another. Both cannot be right.

While pantheism is not mutually exclusive in believing that all roads lead to heaven, its model is just as mutually exclusive as theism and atheism because it carries its own unique truth claim that "all is God." While pantheism is mutually exclusive regarding all religions as equal vehicles to God and heaven, its explanation of the nature of God is completely different from both atheism and theism. Pantheism holds that all religions (as one category) must be included as vehicles to the same spiritual truth. This is just as exclusive as theism and atheism.

THE THREE MAJOR WORLDVIEWS DESCRIBED

PANTHEISM. God is All or God is the Universe. Pantheism is the view that God is everything that is. In other words, pantheism identifies the universe with God. English deist John Toland (1670–1722) first used the term *pantheism* in 1705 when he taught that "God is the mind of the soul of the universe." The problem with pantheism is that it fails to distinguish the Creator from the created, a distinction made clear in the first verse of the Bible: *In the beginning God created the heavens and the earth.*[10]

Hinduism and Buddhism are examples of pantheism. Some years back, I visited a church in Hawaii and asked the pastor about the common theological issues he faced on the island. He told me that one day after he had trimmed the hedges in front of the building, he came outside and found a young man walking up and down the freshly trimmed hedge line, gently stroking the bushes and apologizing to them for the fact that the landscaper did not really understand what he was doing to them. This young man held to a pantheistic worldview, which led him to believe that the hedge plants were literally God since God is all; therefore, the landscaper had just trimmed God.

For the pantheist, there is no Creator beyond the universe. The Creator and creation are two different ways of viewing one reality: God is the universe (or the All) and the universe is God. Since God is seen as an impersonal being embodied in the oneness of the universe, it can be said that God exists within the entirety of all mankind. The Uncaused Cause of theism is not the god of pantheism. Pantheism affirms that an unlimited and necessary being exists but denies the reality of limited and finite beings.[11]

Pantheism is one of the main worldviews that adheres to relativism because it holds that good and evil are illusions. Because good and evil are not real, reality becomes unknown, and therefore not even history can be real. If pantheists were to admit that history does exist, at best it would be cyclical, as depicted in reincarnation.

Pantheists hold to the belief that miracles are not possible in the sense that they are caused by something outside of the world because there is no all-powerful God outside of the universe. Regarding salvation, pantheists believe that our destiny is merely the end goal of uniting with the unknown impersonal God. This union is accomplished through the cycle(s) of reincarnation. And through reincarnation, pantheists strive to reach nirvana or enlightenment, where they finally discover that their existence as an individual being is not real.[12]

ATHEISM. No God exists in or beyond the universe. Simply put, atheism denies that any God exists anywhere. Atheism holds that the universe is eternal. Most secular scientists hold to the belief that the universe came into existence in one moment. They also believe that the Second Law of

Thermodynamics—the belief that the amount of usable energy in the universe is decreasing[13]—scientifically proves that all matter and energy is running down and is not self-perpetuating. The problem for atheism is that if the universe is disconnected from God and all matter and energy is running down, then the universe cannot be eternal. This is very different from the theistic Christian worldview, which holds that the world was created by God out of nothing (*ex nihilo*), and that it is growing old, expending its energy, and winding down in the time-space continuum. Atheists holds the exact opposite view: despite the law of physics and Albert Einstein's Theory of General Relativity, the world is *not* winding down. Their denial is based on the belief that the earth and the entire universe were not wound up in creation by an ultimate Creator, but self-created by random chance by some form of self-perpetuating energy.

The one thing that the atheist still cannot answer is where that energy came from. Atheists believe that the universe was uncaused. To admit to a causal existence is to admit to an Ultimate Eternal Causer, or better yet, a superior being that caused the universe to come into existence. One of the biggest problems that atheists face is that science and logic claim that everything and anything that has been created must have a creator. To deny this notion is to deny logic and the laws of physics. Furthermore, the creator must be bigger than the creation. Is the automaker, the watchmaker, or the maker of the space shuttle greater than the items they created?

Atheists also deny that miracles are possible and that mankind is made in the image of God (Genesis 1:26). They believe that man is a product of random evolutionary chance and processes, which ultimately denies any possibility of life after death. The most extreme form of atheism is found in Marxist communism and by the current Maoist communist philosophy in China. China has schooled over a billion people in the principles of atheism, and most of the Chinese people operate under the assumption that God does not exist. A form of atheism prevalent in the United States is secular humanism, which focuses on the values and interests of human beings. Secular humanism proclaims that man is the measure of all things. Its values are focused on humans, not God.[14]

THEISM. Theism sets forth that an infinite, personal God created the universe and miraculously intervenes in it from time to time. God is both transcendent over the universe and immanent in it. The three great theistic religions—Judaism, Islam, and Christianity—can be distinguished by what they believe about God and his relation to the world. Most theists believe the material world is real, but some believe it exists only in mind and ideas. Most theists believe that God is unchangeable, but some (generally influenced by pantheism) believe God can and does change. Some theists believe it is possible that the created universe is eternal, while most believe the universe must be temporal. Many theists believe that miracles are possible. Although God operates his universe in a regular and orderly way by the laws of nature, nevertheless, God does transcend those laws.

In theism, nature is not the whole story. There is also a supernatural realm, which can invade the natural realm. The sovereign Creator cannot be locked outside his creation. Although God normally works in a regular way, on occasion he directly intervenes. This occasional invasion of nature by the supernatural is called a "miracle."

Perhaps the most important difference among theists is that some, such as Jews and Muslims, believe God is only one person (monotheism). Others, notably orthodox Christians, believe in a Trinitarian form of monotheism: God has three centers of personhood within one perfect monotheistic unity.[15]

To the orthodox Christian, an infinite, personal God exists in and beyond the universe. Furthermore, this personal, infinite God created the physical universe, sustains it, and holds it all together. This theistic God sometimes supernaturally intervenes in the world. The Bible makes this assertion: *And he is before all things, and in him all things hold together* (Colossians 1:17 ESV). In fact, this theistic God will resurrect the dead, and persons will live an immortal and embodied life in the hereafter. This is the view represented by traditional Judaism, Christianity, and Islam.[16]

THE IMPORTANCE OF WORLDVIEW

One's worldview influences and determines personal meaning in life, including moral values. One of the most important questions answered by each worldview is this: where did we come from? This determines whether our morality is based on an absolute good God or on each person's preferences, tastes, and desires. Based on these two choices, all moral questions are answered. For example, should we pull the plug on a severely ill patient in a hospital bed? How do we treat or punish criminals? Our answers to these moral questions stem directly from our worldview.

Pantheism says that we emanated from God like rays from the sun or sparks popping out of a campfire. As a result, pantheists believe that creation is out of God Himself (*ex deo)*. For the pantheist, death is nothing more than a cessation of one's life, which leads to the next life through reincarnation. The ultimate goal of pantheism is to work our way up through millions of years of reincarnation and countless life forms to the point that we are finally merged with God, becoming part of the "Oneness" with all others who have reached nirvana or enlightenment. This Oneness does not involve a personal relationship with God; each person simply merges into the Oneness of God in the form of *Brahman* or *Nirvana.*[17]

Atheism denies the existence of God. It holds to the belief that all creation came out of existing matter (*ex materia)*.[18] More simply, atheism asserts that a bunch of "space junk" came together over millions of years to form the universe, including Planet Earth. But in the end, the atheist still cannot answer one simple question: "Where did the space junk come from?" And who made the space junk? The Jewish Torah and the Christian Bible answer that question decisively: *In the beginning God created the heavens and the earth* (Genesis 1:1).

Christians and Jews are theists. They believe that God created the universe out of nothing, *ex nihilo*. Biblical theists believe God created the human race, meaning you and me, with a purpose, and that purpose included the notion that we would fellowship for eternity with Him. This is the opposite of pantheists, who believe that we lose all individual identity in God as we merge up into Oneness as a part of the whole, like a spoke in a wheel merges into the hub. Atheists see immortality as a carrying on of the human race through the species. Humans live on only in the memory of others for a short period of time and in that way influence the following generations. Once forgotten, a person's impact on future generations becomes thinned out and then nonexistent, apart from the DNA passed on through offspring.[19]

JUDAISM AND CHRISTIANITY: COMPLEMENTARY THEISTIC WORLDVIEWS

Judaism and Christianity fit together like a puzzle, completing one another through the Jewish Torah (which is identical to the Pentateuch—the first five books of the Bible), Old Testament prophecy, and the Christian fulfillment of that prophecy in the New Testament Scriptures. The New Testament cannot be rejected; neither can it stand alone. Together, the Torah, Old Testament prophecy, and the New Testament tell the full story of God's creation as well as his involvement in the world and his people. For example, the Torah and Old Testament point to more than 100 prophesies that are fulfilled in the New Testament.

ISLAM: AN OPPOSITIONAL THEISTIC WORLDVIEW

Islam's holy book, the *Quran*, which means to "recite," claims to be the word-for-word verbally inspired Word of God. Muslims consider it to be authoritative, final, and complete—transmitted to the prophet Muhammad by the angel Gabriel over a period of twenty-three years. Islam's second set of holy writings is the *Hadith* (traditions), which are an account of what the Prophet Muhammad said or did. The Hadith was handed down orally for generations. Many of the traditions are transcribed into *Sharia* (Islamic Law), and are the foundation of Islamic law and government. Islamic law and government are based on the Quran and the Hadith, the

Irma (consensus of the community) and the *Quays* (deduction of new rules).

The Quran treats Judaism and Christianity with a more peaceful attitude in its earlier *Suras*, or chapters, than in its later ones. For example, the early chapters state that there is no compulsion in religion (Sura 2:256), that Jews and Christians are to obey the Bible (Sura 5:68), and that Muhammad said to consult Christians for truth (Sura 10:94). But the later Suras speak more negatively toward Jews and Christians. For example, these Suras command followers to strike off the heads and fingertips of infidels (Sura 8:12), fight them until they are all Muslims (Sura 8:40), strike terror in the hearts of all unbelievers (Sura 8:60), and make war against unbelievers (Sura 9:29). The Quran also requests that Allah destroy Jews and Christians (Sura 9:30). Not all Muslims hold these views.

Although Muslims claim Muhammad is greater than Jesus, an examination of both the Christian and Muslim faiths reveals the opposite. A comparison of the basic beliefs of Muhammad (Islam) to the basic beliefs of Jesus Christ (Christianity) shows that they are one hundred and eighty degrees diametrically opposed. Opposites cannot mean the same thing. Islam claims that Christianity is not a way to heaven, and Christianity claims that Islam is not a way to heaven. Christianity and Islam are so far apart that it renders any notion of pluralistic incorporation impossible. The chart below compares what the New Testament says about Jesus to what the Quran teaches about Muhammad.

MUHAMMAD	JESUS
Not virgin born	Virgin born
Sinful	Sinful
No miracles	Did miracles
Use of the sword to advace religion	Forbids sword to advance religion
Retaliates against enemies	Forgave enemies
Motivated by fear	Motivated by love
Overcome by death	Overcame death

Islam is not simply a religion. It is an inclusive cultural structure that cannot separate religion from the institutions of social provision, government, military, business, and societal behavior. It is theologically impossible for Islam to separate the government and military from organized religion for the simple fact that Islam is a theocracy—a form of government in which God or a deity is recognized as the supreme civil ruler over all society and government authority. Islam is a form of communism based on the Quran and Sharia Law as the authorities over every area of life. This is a major reason Islam's theistic worldview is very different from that of Judaism and Christianity. Worldview is important, and all worldview questions lead to God in one way, shape, or form. That leads us to look at what evidence there is for the existence of God in the first place, which is the subject matter of the next chapter.

CHAPTER 2

DOES GOD EXIST?

By night an atheist half believes a God.[1] —Edward Young

When I think about the three Mount Hood climbers, I wonder about their worldview. Were they thinking about the God who created mountains when they began their ascent up the mountain or when they knew their lives were in jeopardy?

God uses the imagery of mountains and valleys often in his Word to describe his power and give evidence of his existence. Here are a few Scriptures that come to mind:

> *I lift up my eyes to the mountains—where does my help come from? My help comes from the Lord, the Maker of heaven and earth.* (Psalm 121:1–2)
>
> *Before the mountains were born or you brought forth the whole world, from everlasting to everlasting you are God.* (Psalm 90:2)

For since the creation of the world God's invisible qualities—his eternal power and divine nature—have been clearly seen, being understood from what has been made, so that people are without excuse. (Romans 1:20)

Believing in God has consequences. Failure to believe in God also has consequences. Failure to be equipped and be equipped well has consequences that impact your belief in the true God of the universe.

BELIEVING IN GOD HAS CONSEQUENCES

When I first moved to Charlotte, NC, I worked out in a small YMCA on the outskirts of town. At the Y, I've had a sea of opportunity to share my faith in Jesus Christ with a variety of folks ranging from devout Muslims to atheists to people of different sexual orientations. Sometimes the most frustrating conversations are with folks who have no understanding of the truth of gospel, despite having gone to church their entire life.

One lady, with whom I had many meaningful conversations, was a self-proclaimed agnostic from California named Barbara. She and I had more conversations about the existence of God, Jesus Christ, and heaven than I can count. We both enjoyed hearing what one another had to say because we entered the conversation with respect for one another and an open mind. One of our most memorable conversations revolved around the evidence that Christianity is the exclusive truth. Responding to my follow-up question about a book I had given her to read on the subject, Barbara said, "I am stuck on page one—the concept of eternity." Barbara told me that she could not, or in my estimation would not, grasp the concept of infinity. I told her that we cannot fully grasp infinitude because we are not infinite beings. As created, finite beings, we can apprehend the concept of eternality, but we cannot fully understand it because we were created within the time-space continuum, and everything in our universe has both a start and end point.

I concluded that Barbara probably didn't want to accept an infinite Supreme Being (God) as the infinite Creator of the universe. I believe that her obstacle was God Himself. If she accepted the concept of infinitude, she would be accountable to the existence of an infinite being as the only reasonable answer to all creation. For Barbara to allow me to put a crack in her agnostic worldview would have led to changes in her everyday life, both morally and theologically.

The book of Psalms says, *For the Lord is the great God, the great King above all gods. In his hand are the depths of the earth, and the mountain peaks belong to him. The sea is his, for he made it, and his hands formed the dry land. Come,* ***let us bow down in worship****, let us kneel before the* ***Lord our Maker****; for he is our God and we are the people of his pasture* (Psalm 95:3–7 NIV, emphasis added). My sense was that Barbara struggled with connecting God's creation—the things she can see with her eyes and touch with her hands—to faith in God as the Creator whom she cannot perceive with her physical senses.

GOD'S CREATION AND FAITH

God reveals three important truths in the following passage:

> *Now faith is the assurance of things hoped for, the conviction of things not seen.... By faith we understand that the universe was created by the word of God, so that what is seen was not made out of things that are visible.* (Hebrews 11:1–3 ESV)

First, we learn that God "created" the universe. Second, our faith, assurance, and things hoped for are in "the things not seen." Third, the universe was "not made" out of anything; creation was *ex nihilo*, from the Latin meaning, "from out of nothing."[2]

While it is by faith that we understand the universe was created by God, scientific evidence backs the Scriptures. The end result is that our hope is founded in the Creator God as displayed in his creation. I sensed that Barbara was not ready for such life change.

Barbara is not alone. Most of us, at one point or another, have struggled with the existence of God. In fact, one of the smartest people to ever walk the earth, Albert Einstein, struggled with it.

ALBERT EINSTEIN'S STRUGGLE

Albert Einstein initially rejected theism in favor of pantheism. In a 1929 cable reply to Rabbi Goldstein of New York, Einstein described his belief in a pantheistic concept of God, which reflected the view of Benedict Spinoza (1632-1677), a Jewish refugee. Einstein wrote, "I believe in Spinoza's God who reveals himself in the harmony of all that exists, not in a God who concerns himself with the fate and actions of men."[3]

Einstein wrote the general theory of relativity, a mathematical equation showing that the big bang theory was valid—the origin of the universe had to have a beginning because of the evidence of an expanding universe. Einstein's theory created a conflict for his philosophical and theological concept of God because, if the universe is running down, it must have been wound up by something greater. And God is the only plausible explanation. Anything created mandates a creator greater than itself, and the creation of the universe is no exception. It mandates an Ultimate Creator. The problem for Einstein was that the existence of a *theistic* Creator supported the biblical worldview and disproved his pantheistic worldview.

THE FUDGE FACTOR

To appease his pantheistic worldview, Einstein added a "fudge factor"—a series of zeroes—to his theory of relativity. His fudge factor was soon discovered by Russian mathematician Alexander Friedmann, who quickly pointed out the reason for Einstein's omission—a schoolboy's error in algebra. Einstein eventually acknowledged his error in calculation and conceded to Friedmann's results. Einstein admitted, "My objection rested on an error in calculation. I consider Mr. Friedmann's results to be correct and illuminating." However, "this circumstance [of an expanding universe] irritated me."[4]

Why was Einstein irritated? The answer is simple—cognitive dissonance, which is defined as an inconsistent state of beliefs creating tension in one's mind. In other words, Einstein's worldview was ideologically driven by his desire to maintain a pantheistic view of God. The problem for Einstein was that the conclusion of his theory of relativity pointed clearly and inescapably to a theistic God who created the universe. To restore harmony in his mind and still cling to his pantheistic worldview, Einstein added the fudge factor to compartmentalize the truth about what he had discovered regarding God and creation. Einstein eventually embraced the truth: "I am not interested in this or that phenomenon, in the spectrum of this or that element. I want to know his [God's] thought, the rest are details."[5]

FROM DISORDER TO ORDER

As Albert Einstein discovered through his general law of relativity, the universe was created, or came into existence, in a single moment as depicted in the book of Genesis, chapters one and two. WORLD magazine's digital daily news report, *The Sift*, reported on October 3, 2017, that "Einstein's academic heirs win physics Nobel Prize." Three scientists, based in the USA, won the Nobel Physics Prize for detecting the gravitational waves rippling through space as Albert Einstein had predicted. This discovery energized the scientific world because it confirmed Einstein's theory of relativity, which asserts that 3-D space and time are woven together in a single continuum. This is called a *fabric,* which can stretch, shrink, and tremble.

What is the significance of their discovery? The existence of gravitational waves confirms what creationist Jeff Zweerink, an astrophysicist at UCLA, claims: "If general relativity is correct, that implies there is a beginning to the universe, and if there is a beginning, then there is a beginner." This discovery is confirmed by reputable sources, including Rainer Weiss, a German-born American physicist at the Massachusetts Institute of Technology, and Barry Barish and Kip Thorne of the California Institute of Technology, who share the Nobel Prize for the discovery.[6] While the universe came into existence in a single moment, God took time (how much time depends on your view of the earth's age), filling out the universe—taking disorder into order.

- On the first day of creation, God takes the watery, formless Planet Earth, which was suspended in the darkness and void of space—no sun, other stars, moon, or planets existed. On that day, he adds light, then separates light from the darkness through the planet's rotation.
- On the second day, God forms the earth's atmosphere, separating the water into two parts—oceanic and atmospheric water.
- On the third day, God creates dry land and defines bodies of water called oceans. He also creates a system to water the entire land surface using subterranean waters through springs, mist, rain, etc. On day three, he also creates vegetation, seed-bearing plants, and fruit-bearing trees. The Garden of Eden may also have been created on the third day.
- On the fourth day, God creates the sun, moon, and the stars.
- On the fifth day, God creates creatures to live in the water and birds that fly in the air.
- On the sixth day, he creates land animals and creatures that move close to the ground—small and large animals. On this day, God also creates the first human beings, man (Adam) and woman (Eve). Mankind is the only created being made in God's own image: *So God created mankind in his own image, in the image of God he created him; male and female he created them* (Genesis 1:27).

FROM ORDER TO DISORDER

Have you ever noticed that when your life veers from God's Word, his ways, and his will, that your life slides into a state of disorder? God created the universe, the earth, and the human race in a perfect order. In the book of Matthew, chapter twelve, Jesus tells us about God's order and Satan's disorder:

> *When an impure spirit comes out of a person, it goes through arid places seeking rest and does not find it. Then it says, "I will return to*

> *the house I left." When it arrives, it finds the house unoccupied, swept clean and* put in order. *Then it goes and takes with it seven other spirits more wicked than itself, and they go in and live there. And the final condition of that person is worse than the first. That is how it will be with this wicked generation.* (Matthew 12:43–45)

God brings order and evil creates disorder. Taking God's order to disorder started in the Garden of Eden with Adam and Eve. The serpent in Eden—the fallen angel, Satan—is a creature of disorder. Adam and Eve sinned, taking God's perfectly created physical and moral order to a state of physical and moral disorder.

Fast forward to the Tower of Babel in Genesis 11 where man, through his own strengths and merits, attempts to regain control of God. As a result, God ultimately sends his only Son Jesus Christ into the disorder man created to eliminate the sting of death and restore order once and for all. Through the atoning sacrifice of Christ on the cross, God takes mankind from a state of sin, disorder, and death under the judgment of God, and puts creation back on track for a life of order.

THE FIRST AND SECOND LAWS OF THERMODYNAMICS

How God took creation from disorder to order is explained in the book of Genesis. And science backs up the Genesis account of creation. On its homepage, entropylaw.com opens with this heading: All about Entropy, the Laws of Thermodynamics, and Order from Disorder.[7] Entropylaw.com states that "the law of entropy, or the second law of thermodynamics, along with the first law of thermodynamics comprise the most fundamental laws of physics."[8] Entropy, the focus of the second law of thermodynamics, and energy, the subject of the first law are essential to understanding life and order. The first and second laws of thermodynamics are important because they hold important implications for creationism.

The first law states that the amount of actual energy in the universe remains constant, but it says nothing about how the energy came into existence. The second law states that in a closed, isolated system, such as the universe, the amount of usable energy in the universe is decreasing. Clear as mud? Okay, let me put it more simply. The first law says constant energy is found within the universe. This includes the burning stars, such as the sun, among other things. The second law states that within an isolated system, such as the universe, this energy is decreasing. In other words, energy from the sun and other stars, for example, is diminishing. Yes, one day the sun will burn out, but not in the near future.

These two laws hold important implications for creationists for two reasons: (1) The first law does not say anything about how that energy came into existence; (2) because all energy is decreasing according to the second law, some supreme power must have created that energy. The only rational answer here is the existence of God as proclaimed in the Bible: *In the beginning God created the heavens and the earth. Now the earth was formless and empty, darkness was over the surface of the deep, and the Spirit of God was hovering over the waters* (Genesis 1:1–2).

From Adam and Eve to Einstein to Jesus Christ, we see mankind's struggle to dismiss or minimize the existence of God in an attempt to make God smaller and mankind larger. In the process, mankind forfeits an ordered relationship with God and instead embraces an increasingly sinful world of disorder. While this is a moral issue, which will be covered in the chapter on moral relativism, it is pertinent here to understand that God exists, which is made evident not only in his moral order but also in his created order as seen both in the cosmos and in its design.

PROOF ARGUMENTS FOR GOD'S EXISTENCE

Our hope in the Creator God is displayed in his creation, so let's now turn our attention to three proof arguments for the existence of God as seen through his creation, his design of the universe, and his ability to sustain the universe. These three arguments are known as the Cosmological Argument, the Design Argument (or Teleological Argument), and the Moral Argument.

THE COSMOLOGICAL ARGUMENT

1) The universe had a beginning.
2) Anything that had a beginning must have been caused by something else.
3) Therefore, the universe was caused by something else, which we call God.[9]

Scientists believed that the universe was eternal up until the 1920s when astronomer Edwin Hubble discovered the universe was expanding. Expansion implies a beginning. A beginning mandates a Supreme Beginner Maker-God. About a decade after Einstein's theory of relativity, legendary astronomer Edwin Hubble looked through his telescope and scientists finally confirmed not only that the universe is expanding but also that it is expanding from a single point. That single point is not the size of a basketball, a baseball, or even a pinhead—but out of nothing. If we could watch a video of the recorded history of the universe in reverse, we could see all matter in the universe collapse back to a single point of nothingness (i.e., no space, no time, and no matter). In other words, the big bang occurred and then there was something—the entire universe exploded into existence. These facts give atheists a lot of trouble because this cosmological-scientific evidence points clearly to the existence of God.[10]

WHAT THEN DID GOD CREATE THE UNIVERSE OUT OF?

While there can only be one truth as to what the universe was created out of, three philosophies attempt to give the answer:

1) **EX MATERIA** (*out of existing space junk/material*)
2) **EX DEO** (*out of God*)
3) **EX NIHILO** (*out of nothing*)

The problem with *ex materia*, or creation out of existing space junk/material, is that it raises this question: who then created the space junk or material found in outer space? As we noted at the beginning of the chapter, Hebrews 11:3 says, *By faith we understand that the universe was created by the word of God, so that what is seen was not made out of things that are visible* (ESV). Notice that the universe was created *from* the word of God, not *out of* the word of God. Furthermore, the Word was God. *In the beginning was the Word, and the Word was with God, and the Word was God* (John 1:1).

The problem with *ex deo*, or out of God, is that God is pure spirit. Jesus tells us in the book of Luke that spirit has no finite, material properties such as flesh and bones: *"See my hands and my feet, that it is I myself. Touch me, and see. For a spirit does not have flesh and bones as you see that I have"* (Luke 24:39 ESV). The verse from Hebrews, cited in the previous paragraph, says that *what is seen was not made out of things that are visible.* The book of John tells us, *God is spirit, and those who worship him must worship in spirit and truth* (John 4:24 ESV). Lastly, if *material* things were to come *out of* God, it would mandate that God is made in part or whole out of material matter. But pure spirit has no finite, material component. God is simple, spiritual being.

The word *ex nihilo* comes from the Latin, meaning "from out of nothing." The theistic view of origins affirms that God brought the universe into existence without using preexisting material. Only theism declares that God is eternal and that he brought everything else into being without the existence of preexisting material or out of pieces of his own substance. To do so would have been impossible because God is pure spirit. Therefore, the universe was made from nothing, *ex nihilo.*[11]

IF GOD CREATED THE UNIVERSE, WHO CREATED GOD?

Most people agree that every created thing has a beginning and is caused by something greater than itself as opposed to popping into existence out of thin air. This is true of every single thing within the space-time continuum and the universe. The exception is God. Why? He is the only being who exists outside of the space-time continuum. Because God has always existed (is eternal), he is outside the space-time continuum and therefore is not subject to finite time. While time is a series of moments within the created universe, time is a measurement of limited moments. God is the eternal, uncaused cause of all things outside himself.

Before heading to Egypt to tell Pharaoh to let God's people go free, Moses asks God what name he should give the Israelites for the God who is about to free them from slavery. In response, God says, "*I AM WHO I AM* [is going to set them free]. *This is what you are to say to the Israelites: 'I AM has sent me to you'*" (Exodus 3:14).

I AM has always been my favorite name for God because it speaks to his eternal nature. God has neither a past nor a future. He simply IS because he is eternal. As I told my atheist friend Barbara, we are finite, created beings, so our minds cannot fully grasp what it is like to be eternal. However, we can apprehend the concept of eternality—which applies only to God. The Bible proclaims that truth in both the Old and New Testaments: *Before the mountains were born ... from everlasting to everlasting you are God* (Psalm 90:2); *for every house is built by someone, but God is the builder of everything* (Hebrews 3:4).

This leads us to the second argument for the existence of God, the Design Argument, which shows that a designer must exist for intelligent life to exist.

THE DESIGN (TELEOLOGICAL) ARGUMENT:

1) Every design had a designer.
2) The universe has a highly complex design.
3) Therefore, the universe had a Designer.[12]

Cambridge-trained English apologist and theologian William Paley (1743–1805) gave us the design argument in *Argument for God's Existence*.[13] He came up with the infamous watch analogy: If someone found a watch in an empty field, he would rightly conclude that it had a maker because of its obvious design.[14] Likewise, when one looks at the even more complex design of the world in which we live, one cannot but conclude that there is a great Designer behind it. [15]

How many millions of times would you have to throw down a piece of leather, some metal scraps, and glass shards before they arranged themselves into a functioning wrist watch that tells accurate time? The answer is obvious: No matter how many times you did it, you could never create a watch that way. A watch, like any other thing, mandates a creator greater than itself.

THE DESIGN ARGUMENT FROM BIOLOGY AND DNA

The argument for the existence of God from design is made abundantly clear with our modern understanding of DNA. Our DNA is too complex to credit random design over millions or billions of years.

Atheists and theists acknowledge that the universe and life have the appearance of design rather than the appearance of formation by chance. We know that anything created mandates something greater than itself as its creator. This is made evident in our DNA, which is like computer code. The volume of DNA is roughly equivalent to twelve sets of the *Encyclopedia Britannica*, all 384 volumes. This is significant because all known codes and languages were created by an intelligent agent, not by chance—including DNA.

DNA SUPPORTS BIBLICAL SCRIPTURE

Leading modern-day DNA evidence confirms the biblical account of Adam and Eve. *Answers in Genesis'* Georgia Purdom released a documentary explaining her findings and scientific support for the Genesis account of creation. In it, Purdom points to leading creation geneticist Dr. Nathaniel Jeanson, who says, "One of the most compelling genetic evidences for an original human couple created by God is mitochondrial DNA research done by creation geneticist, Dr. Nathaniel Jeanson." Purdom says in her findings that "he [Dr. Jeanson] shows that the common human female ancestor of us all [biblical Eve] lived within the biblical timeframe of several thousand years ago."

Jeanson is saying that if evolution were true and men and women had been roaming the planet for millions of years, there would be much more genetic diversity. With all the modern advancements in DNA, scientists have been able to evaluate the origin of men and women, tracing their roots back to a man and a woman. Jeanson's evidence, although not his timeline, coincides with a study claiming that all men can trace their lineage to a single man who lived 135,000 years ago—a "Genetic Adam."

Jeanson also says, "The Y chromosome is passed down identically from father to son, so mutations, or point changes, in the male sex chromosome can trace the male line back to the father of all humans." In "Genetic 'Adam' and 'Eve' Uncovered," Live Science's Tia Ghose writes that "by contrast, DNA from the mitochondria, the energy powerhouse of the cell, is carried inside the egg, so only women pass it on to their children. The DNA hidden inside mitochondria, therefore, can reveal the maternal lineage of an ancient Eve."

WHY DNA IS IMPORTANT TO THE BIBLICAL ACCOUNT OF CREATION

Jessilyn Justice brings this all together by answering why this is so important to the biblical account of creation, the validity of the Holy Bible, and our faith in Jesus Christ. For creationists, the scientific evidence backs both the existence of Adam and Eve as well as the truth of Genesis. It also provides overwhelming support for the need of a Savior (Jesus Christ) in a broken world. In a world devoid of Adam, Eve, and original sin, Purdom says, we would not need a Savior, and salvation would be unnecessary. If salvation were unnecessary, then the need for the atonement of sins by Jesus Christ on the cross at Calvary would not be necessary either. Genetic research consistently proves the case for Christ, not just creation. Purdom goes on to say, "We need the good news, grace, and life, which is found in the death and resurrection of Jesus Christ.... Jesus is the solution for the problem of evil that began in Genesis chapter three."

This adds emphasis to two upcoming chapters, "Did Jesus Really Rise from the Dead?" and "Why Does God Allow Bad Things to Happen to Good People?"

In addition to the fine-tuning of our individual DNA is the fine-tuning of the earth and the universe. God both created and designed the universe with great precision, and his design is made abundantly clear in what has come to be known as the Anthropic Principle.

FIVE FINE-TUNINGS OF THE UNIVERSE AND THE ANTHROPIC PRINCIPLE

The anthropic principle states that the universe was fitted from the first moment of its existence for the emergence of life in general and human life in particular. American astronomer and planetary physicist Robert Jastrow, who founded the Goddard Institute for Space Studies, noted that the universe is amazingly pre-adapted to the eventual appearance of humanity. Jastrow, an agnostic at that time, was referring to the fine-tuning and design of the universe and everything in it.

For example, on earth, we breathe air comprised of 78.09 percent nitrogen, 20.95 percent oxygen, with the remaining 1 percent of air comprised of argon and carbon dioxide, among other elements. Human beings need this precise combination to live on earth. Furthermore, Planet Earth needs these same precise percentages in effort to function without imploding. Note the following facts:

1) Oxygen comprises 21 percent of the atmosphere. If oxygen comprised 25 percent instead of 21 percent of the atmosphere, fires would erupt; if the atmosphere were only 15 percent oxygen, humans would suffocate.
2) If the fine-tuned gravitational force were altered by one part in ten to the fortieth power (forty zeros), the sun would not exist and the moon would crash into the earth.
3) If Jupiter were not in its current orbit, we would be bombarded with space material, because Jupiter acts like a vacuum cleaner for

asteroids and other space junk.

4) If the rotation of the earth took longer than twenty-four hours—daytime temperature differences would be too great between day and night. If the rotation of the earth were shorter than twenty-four hours, the atmospheric wind velocities would be too great.
5) If the tilt of the earth were off just a few degrees, temperature differences would be so fierce that all life on Planet Earth would either freeze or burn up.

The evidence for the existence of God is found in his creation, the cosmos, and his design of the cosmos and all created things. This is evident in the way the entire universe is laid out and fine-tuned. While these two arguments (Cosmological and Teleological) are based on what is around us, the third argument—the Moral Argument for the existence of God—considers knowledge that is inside us.

THE MORAL ARGUMENT FOR GOD

The moral argument for God will be covered more thoroughly in an upcoming chapter on moral relativism. The moral argument states the objective standards (an Ultimate Moral Law) exist outside of personal opinion. The best explanation for the existence of those standards is the existence of a Moral Lawgiver such as God. The formal argument states:

1) Every law has a lawgiver.
2) There is an ultimate Moral Law.
3) Therefore, there is an ultimate Moral Lawgiver.

WHAT DOES SCRIPTURE SAY ABOUT AN ULTIMATE MORAL LAW?

Scripture is clear that God gives us the Ultimate Moral Law. The apostle James tells us in chapter four of his book, *There is only one Lawgiver and Judge, the one who is able to save and destroy. But you—who are you to judge your neighbor?* (James 4:12). While James is speaking to us as believers about judging one another, notice the moral measuring stick is God, not a human being. In the book of Romans, the apostle Paul proclaims that even though God gave the Jewish people both his written and moral law, the gentiles also have God's moral law written on their hearts:

> *Indeed, when Gentiles, who do not have the law, do by nature things required by the law, they are a law for themselves, even though they do not have the law. They show that the requirements of the law are written on their hearts, their consciences also bearing witness, and their thoughts sometimes accusing them and at other times even defending them.* (Romans 2:14–15)

The interaction of conscience and innate morality may result in a good life. To such persons God sends the gospel (Acts 4:12; Romans 10:4).

SUMMARY

I can't help but wonder about the faith of the Mount Hood climbers. Had they placed their faith in God or in self? Did they gaze at the magnificence of Mount Hood and see a challenge easily attained by human will and grit, or did they approach the mountain in awe of the One who created it? I don't have a definitive answer because I have not read anything pertaining to the faith of any of the three climbers. Furthermore, the fact is that they packed lightly with the miscalculated confidence they would get up and down the mountain without any major obstacles. This gross miscalculation cost them their lives.

As I think back to my conversations with my YMCA friend Barbara, I realize that she saw the same things that I saw—things every human being in the universe sees—the overwhelming evidence for the existence of God in the cosmos, the design of the universe, and the ultimate moral code. Barbara's obstacle was not the fine tuning of the universe but the fine tuning of her theological belief in God in light of the immense data and evidence that supports the Genesis account of creation.

Barbara was a liberal Jewish agnostic, so I often referred to the Torah (identical to the first five books of the Bible). When speaking to her about God and creation, I often quoted from other Old Testament Scriptures, including the book of Psalms (also contained in Hebrew Scriptures). For example, Psalm 74 says, *It was you [God] who opened up the springs and streams; you dried up the ever-flowing rivers. The day is yours, and yours also the night; you established the sun and the moon. It was you who set all the boundaries of the earth; you made both summer and winter* (vv. 15–17).

I also bridged parts of the Old Testament/Torah with the New Testament Scriptures. For example, God tells us through the apostle Paul that we as human beings have no excuse for denying that God is the creator of the universe because it has been made abundantly evident to all of us:

> *Since what may be known about God is plain to them, because God has made it plain to them. For since the creation of the world God's invisible qualities—his eternal power and divine nature—have been clearly seen, being understood from what has been made, so that men are without excuse.* (Romans 1:19–20)

In other words, the evidence of his creation (universe) is clear to all human beings in all cultures. Scripture states that mankind is without excuse because things that are made (creation) reveal to all mankind the "eternal power and divine nature" of the true God. Therefore, the rejection of this truth makes a man or woman "without excuse" before God.

Apologetics is a tool in our toolbox to help remove obstacles that keep us from accepting the truth about God found in Scripture, to equip us to share the truth of God with others, and to strengthen our own faith in him. God created the universe, and our faith is the assurance of things hoped for and the conviction of things not seen (Hebrews 11:1–3). The universe was not made out of anything seen but by the word of God. Therefore, God's creation is *ex nihilo*, from the Latin meaning, "from out of nothing" (materially speaking).

Barbara's reluctance to even grapple seriously with the concept of infinity was probably an excuse for her to avoid coming face to face with the true God of the universe—the God of her ancestors. I shared the truth about God through her own holy book, the Torah, the New Testament Scriptures, and the overwhelming evidence that supports the existence of an Ultimate Creator God:

1) The creation of the cosmos (creation of the universe and everything in it)
2) Evidence from his extremely detailed design of the universe, Planet Earth, the stars and other planets, and us as human beings
3) Through the fact that people in all cultures share a common basic moral law which can only be explained by the existence of an Ultimate Moral Lawgiver, God.

Astronomer Robert Jastrow ends his book *God and the Astronomers* with a telling line about the agnostic's fear of the evidence from God's design: "For the scientist who has lived by his faith in the power of reason, the story ends like a bad dream. He has scaled the mountains of ignorance; he is about to conquer the highest peak; as he pulls himself over the final rock, he is greeted by a band of theologians who have been sitting there for centuries."

The onus is on Barbara to take what she knows to be true about God and apply it to life and her worldview. The foundation for the existence of God leads to another question: do all religions lead to the same God? That is the subject of the next chapter.

Chapter 3

COEXIST: DO ALL RELIGIOUS ROADS LEAD TO HEAVEN?

To believe in God is to yearn for his existence and, furthermore, it is to act as if he did exist.[1] —Miguel de Unamuno

Another woman I got to know at the YMCA is Cheryl. Over time, I learned that her grandfather was a strong Christian who had been tied closely to the slave era and that her grandmother was a Native American. When I asked Cheryl about her religious beliefs, she told me she was a Christian.

After we had known each other about three years, a news story came up on the TV screen one day at the YMCA about Islam and religious exclusivity. Cheryl said she did not understand the problem. Her statement perplexed me, so I asked her to clarify what she meant. Cheryl said she believed that both Islam and Christianity lead to the same God and the same heaven. I asked her the question another way because I thought she had misstated her belief. She replied, "It is arrogant to think that Christ is the *only way* to heaven." I kindly told her that, according to the Bible, the exclusive deity of Christ and the belief that he is the only way to heaven are essential to Christianity. To say otherwise is to disqualify oneself from being a Christian and from eternal salvation. I then attempted to assure her that we were still friends.

Cheryl did not like my insistence on the basic tenets of Christianity, so she reported me to the YMCA's main office. When a YMCA staff person questioned me about the incident, I replied, "I am flexible about many things but not about the exclusive deity of the Lord Jesus Christ." I tried to remain Cheryl's friend to be a witness to her, but she chose to remain bitter. I wish that Cheryl had been able to coexist with me even though my beliefs differed from hers, but she was intolerant to the point of never speaking to me again. Cheryl's attitude illustrates the hypocrisy of the coexist mantra.

THE COEXIST BUMPER STICKER

Have you ever passed a car with a COEXIST bumper sticker or seen someone wearing a shirt that had the coexist symbols on it? While this mantra proposes to promote coexistence and tolerance among people of different faiths, it conveys the inclusive message that all of us should embrace every religion as a valid belief system leading to the same God and a generic place called heaven. A common rendition of the coexist design is made up of the following symbols:

- For the letter C, a crescent moon representing Islam is substituted.
- For the letter O, the peace symbol or pagan/Wiccan pentacle is substituted.
- For the letter E, a male/female symbol or a scientific equation is substituted.
- For the letter X, the Star of David representing Judaism is substituted.
- For the letter I, a representation of an *ankh* for ancient Egyptian re-

ligions, modern for neo-pagans as a symbol of strength and wisdom.

- For the letter S, a Chinese yin-yang symbol is substituted.
- For the letter T, a cross representing Christianity is substituted.

Some of the original coexist sketches/bumper stickers focused on harmony between the three monotheistic faiths of Judaism, Christianity, and Islam. More recent sketches expanded to include the New Age earth-centered symbol, the yin-yang symbol for Eastern religions, the peace sign, and the gender signs representing homosexuality and cross-gender.

While we live in a global world with many worldviews and belief systems, the coexist mantra communicates much more than promoting interfaith dialog; it communicates that all religions and worldviews lead to the same place, generically called heaven. The original intent of the COEXIST bumper sticker may have been to instill respect for and to promote the dignity of people of all faiths and worldviews. But its message now boldly proclaims inclusivity—that all religions lead to the same spiritual truth despite the fact that each religion says it holds the exclusive claim to truth. In America, tolerance has always allowed for all religions and worldviews to coexist, find common ground, and learn from each other. If that were not true, there would be very little representation of other religions and worldviews in American culture. However, mosques, Hindu and Buddhist temples, and Universal churches are among the many houses of worship spread across America.

While we live on a very spiritual and religious planet, many people still do not know the true God of the Bible or of biblical Christianity. Therefore, twenty-first-century Christians must be equipped on three levels:

1) We must know why we believe what we believe.
2) We must be equipped to defend the truth about God and biblical Christianity.
3) We must be equipped to reach our multicultural world to advance the exclusive truth about God, the good news of the Christian faith, and the gift of salvation available to every person in every category of the COEXIST bumper sticker as mandated in the Great Commission (Matthew 28:18–20).

Being equipped will help us know why we believe what we believe and will also remove the blindfold of the coexist proclamation regarding the inclusivity of all religions as truth.

SIX BLIND MEN AND AN ELEPHANT

In a well-known Indian fable, six blind men go into the jungle to examine an elephant that is quietly basking in the summer sun. Each man is told to touch what is directly in front of him. When asked what they believed they were touching, the men responded as follows:

- The man who touched the elephant's trunk said it was a snake.
- The man who touched the elephant's tusk said it was a spear.
- The man who touched the elephant's leg said it was a tree trunk.
- The man who touched the elephant's tail said it was a rope.
- The man who touched the elephant's side believed it was a wall.
- The man who touched the elephant's ear said it was a fan.

The men were arguing about which answer was correct when a wise man stopped by and calmly explained, "All of you are right. The reason each of you tells it differently is because each of you touched a different part of the elephant. The elephant has all the features that all of you described."

This story illustrates the concept of religious pluralism: "the belief that every religion is true and that each provides a genuine encounter with the Ultimate. While one may be better than the other, all religions are adequate."[2] Thus, in this view, all religions hold truth even if this truth is only partially correct—just as the six blind men were only partially correct. Religious pluralism also claims that all religions provide the way to the desired eternal state. No one religion, then—not Judaism, Hinduism, Islam, Christianity, Taoism, or Buddhism—can claim to be exclusively true.[3]

But what if the blind men suddenly could see? Would their perspective of the elephant become clearer? Of course. Many people choose to be blind about spiritual matters. We do not want to be convicted by the truth about God. If we can remain blind to God's existence, we can ignore the truth about his existence, and we do not have to believe in Jesus.[4]

Consider the gospel of John's account of the man who was born blind. Note his sudden transformation: *They brought to the Pharisees the man who had formerly been blind. Now it was a Sabbath day when Jesus made the mud and opened his eyes. So the Pharisees again asked him how he had received his sight. And he said to them, "He put mud on my eyes, and I washed, and I see"* (John 9:13–15 ESV). This man was clearly elated that he could see, yet many of us do not want our eyes opened.

In the biblical account, the Pharisees did not want to believe Jesus' miraculous sign—evidence that he was God. They kept asking the blind man how he was able to see because they did not want to believe it: *A second time they summoned the man who had been blind. "Give glory to God by telling the truth," they said. "We know this man [Jesus] is a sinner." He [the blind man] replied, "Whether he [Jesus] is a sinner or not, I don't know. One thing I do know. I was blind but now I see!"* (John 9:24–25).

If the six blind men could see as the man Jesus healed could see, they would see the whole elephant. They also would realize there is a vast difference between their blind understanding and the truth. Also noteworthy is the fact that the blind men were able to coexist despite their differing worldviews.

IS COEXISTENCE POSSIBLE?

Can all religions coexist? Of course they can! They have done so for thousands of years. And often they coexist peacefully. But if one subscribes to the notion that all religions are equal, and there is no single theistic God who sets rules and boundaries, then mankind becomes the measure of all things. If we choose to believe that mankind is the measure of all things, we end up with totalitarianism and war. Why? Because the only thing keeping one population of humans from conquering other populations of humans is the ultimate standard for goodness found in the true Creator God. This ultimate standard for goodness, though, needs to be of God not of man. We live in an expanding global society that increasingly desires to create a one-world governmental order. We see this in the modern form of the United Nations. This, in turn, is threading the way for a one-world coexist religion and the New Age Movement.

Due to the intense pressure from the political-correctness movement and the misguided interfaith movement, our culture and the marketplace are facing the global threat of the New Age Movement (NAM). This movement is made up of a broad coalition of various organizations that believe in the New World Order centered on a pantheistic (God is all) worldview. Hinduism, Zen Buddhism, Hinduism, and NAM are the major religious movements that adhere to pantheism. NAM believes in a New World Order and a New Age Christ who is very different from biblical Christianity's Christ. NAM's name derives from astrology in that its believers claim that a new age of peace and harmony will replace the current world system. This is the major thrust behind the widespread intolerance toward Christians who hold to an inclusive view of Jesus as the single way to heaven.

Many other names have been used for NAM, such as Human Potential Movement and Holistic Health Movement. Symbols used to represent NAM include the rainbow, pyramid, triangle, eye in triangle, unicorn, and Pegasus.[5] The movement includes many beliefs, ranging from Wicca to witchcraft to Neo-Hinduism to nominal Christianity.

One of the most visible examples of this inclusivity is NAM and positive thinking. NAM views positive thinking as something that establishes control of a person's external being or life through his or her own power. A number of Christian preachers on television and in pulpits deliver messages steeped in positive thinking. What's not to like about feeling good about yourself and controlling life in the name of Christianity? The problem increases as well-meaning Christians substitute biblical principles—such as waiting on God, knowing what is best for our lives, and the value of suffering—for the false NAM belief that self-centered positive thinking, and therefore the ability to control our lives, is in our hands. God becomes a Santa Claus—giving us the okeydokey based on our desires. New Age writer Lord Maitreya is considered by some to be the New Age Christ. Maitreya teaches that one ought not to fear because all Light and Truth lie within each heart, and man will become God once he realizes this.[6]

NAM has been called the fastest growing alternative belief system in the country. Some years ago, sociologists at the University of California–Santa Barbara estimated that as many as twelve million Americans were active NAM participants, and another thirty million were very interested. A large segment of the American population is involved in some form of New Age occultism.[7] New Ager Marilyn Ferguson says, "If all these people were brought together in a church-like organization, it would be the largest religious denomination in America."[8] The New Age Movement is in a class by itself. It has no holy text, central organization, ordained clergy, or geographic center. It is made up of a network of believers and practitioners who share similar beliefs.[9] A survey by George Barna, titled "The Index of Leading Spiritual Indicators," found that 11 percent believe that God is a state of higher consciousness that a person may reach. Furthermore, 8 percent define God as the total realization of personal, human potential, and 3 percent believe that each person is God. The study concluded that 20 percent of the population is New Agers, making them consistently the third largest religious group.[10]

The difference between the New Age Christ and the biblical Jesus Christ is that the biblical Christ proves to be authentic by his uniqueness. By denying that Christ was unique among all other gods, NAM attempts to minimize Christ, reducing him to the level of other gods. If we make Jesus Christ equal—merely one among all other gods—then Christianity and the Bible become equal among all other religions. As a result, the concept of God becomes relative. Another by-product of the intense pressure from the political correctness movement and the misguided interfaith movement is NAM's attempt to make Jesus into a non-unique, religiously pluralistic leader rather than the Son of God.

Conversely, if Jesus Christ and Christianity are the truth, Jesus is unique among all other religious figures in all cultures throughout history.

IS JESUS UNIQUE?

According to NAM, Jesus Christ is not unique. If he is not unique, then he is the same as all other finite humans who have ever walked the earth. This makes it easier to justify man as a god. According to NAM, all people have innate divinity with the potential to become Christ(s). In other words, all people are divine in the same way Christ is divine. NAM points out that Christ was the most advanced human being ever to walk Planet Earth, but he is not God. He is merely a divine being.

Furthermore, NAM puts Jesus Christ and Lucifer on the same level in that Lucifer's role is to create light through the presence of experience and feelings while Christ's role is to move out and to release that light. Christ is to release love and wisdom into creation. David Spangler, author of the New Age book *Reflections on the Christ*, wrote, "Christ is the same force as Lucifer but moving in seemingly the opposite direction. Lucifer moves in to create the light within through the pressure of experience. Christ moves out to release that light, that wisdom, that love into creation."[11] In light of the yin-yang premise, NAM's belief system mandates a balance between the two. Such thought denounces the uniqueness of Christ. This leads us to evaluate what the Bible says about the uniqueness of Christ as compared to NAM.[12]

WHAT DOES THE BIBLE SAY ABOUT THE UNIQUENESS OF JESUS CHRIST?

The Bible is clear about who Jesus Christ is and what he taught. The biblical person of Jesus Christ is very different from, and in direct contrast to, the person of Jesus Christ portrayed by NAM. Scripture is clear that Jesus Christ is unique in nature as the only incarnation of God (John 1:1, 14) as well as the one and only Savior of the world (John 3:16,

18; Philippians 2:1–8; 1 John 2:2).[13] Jesus Christ is more than a mortal man as NAM portrays him. Jesus Christ is not a person who attained Christhood as others can achieve Christhood.

Jesus often proclaimed his uniqueness. For example, he said, *"I am the bread of life. Whoever comes to me will never grow hungry, and whoever believes in me will never be thirsty"* (John 6:35). Jesus said, *"While I am in the world, I am the light of the world"* (John 9:5). Jesus said that he is the gate through which one can be saved for eternity (John 10:9). Finally, Jesus proclaimed that he and God the Father are one (John 10:30). Other supportive Scriptures include John 11:25 and John 14:6.

Jesus proved that he is the truth by fulfilling more than one hundred ancient prophecies, by living a sinless life, by his death on the cross, and by his resurrection from the dead. No other religious leader or figure did this!

There are many ways to Christ, but Christ is the only way to God. Therefore, the Bible is 100 percent right, and the progressive physics of religious pluralism are wrong.

JESUS, THE ONLY WAY TO GOD

While religious pluralism, in general, challenges the biblical claim that Jesus Christ is the only way to God the Father and to heaven, its challenge fails to hold weight. Jesus claimed to be the only way, and he proved in three miraculous ways that he truly is the only way to God.

First, Jesus satisfied God's unchanging call for justice. God's requirement for eternal life has never changed because he never changes his standard of righteousness. Righteousness is one of the chief attributes of God. *The Lord is righteous in all his ways and faithful in all he does* (Psalm 145:17). In other words, it is impossible for God not to demand justice in all and every instance of injustice. It was Jesus who gave his life freely to satisfy God's required payment for our iniquities. Because of Jesus' substitutionary death, we are made right, or justified, before God as if we have never sinned.

Second, we, as sinful beings cannot answer God's call for justice apart from Christ. Jesus Christ's absolute righteousness alone is able to satisfy (propitiate) the just demands of an absolutely righteous God. It is impossible for sinful man to satisfy God's justice on his own. Furthermore, Christ's righteousness is credited (imputed) to those who believe in him as the only way to fulfill the righteous demands of the law (Romans 8:3–4).[14] It is our inability to answer that call that leads us to Jesus Christ, who can. No human being outside of Jesus Christ lived a perfect life, which makes it impossible for any of us to satisfy God's perfect justice. To think otherwise is to put your faith in a counterfeit Christ, which will lead to a counterfeit salvation.[15]

EACH RELIGION HAS A UNIQUE IDENTITY

Religious pluralists, as noted earlier in this chapter, believe that all religions are equal and lead to the same place. The only problem is that all religions reject this notion. Religious pluralism, then, is self-defeating and intolerant.

Pluralism also denies the First Principles of Logic. For example, let's apply pluralism to the Law of Identity, which states that a thing must be identical to itself or it would not be itself. Therefore, a religion must be identical to itself, or it would not be itself. Any religion without a unique identity cannot exist as its own religion, because without that unique identity, it would not be. To exist is to exist as something, that is, to exist with a particular identity. Christianity exists due to its unique correlation to the truth, traditions, and beliefs.[16] The same can be said for Judaism, Islam, and Hinduism. To have an identity means to have a single identity; an object or a religion cannot have two identities. A tree cannot be a telephone. Neither can Christianity be Islam nor can Hinduism be Christianity.

The claim that all religions ultimately lead to the same spiritual truth still connotes an exclusive claim of a singular truth, and this denies the possibility of any plurality of beliefs by its very definition. Logic mandates that there must be one truth, and the one truth makes all others definitions of God and paths to God false.

The coexist mantra, therefore, is self-defeating in its claim that all religions are expressions of the same truth. By looking closely at each religion's beliefs, we can see the glaring contradictions that disqualify their culmination as a single religion.

The Law of Identity makes clear that each reltigion and each god has its own identity. This point is illustrated below in the simple comparisons of the basic but essential beliefs of Islam and Christianity as well as Hinduism and Christianity.[17]

ISLAM	CHRISTIANITY
God: Only one person	**God:** Three persons in one God (Triune God)
Humanity: Good by nature **Jesus:** Merely a man	**Humanity:** Sinful by nature **Jesus:** More than a man; He was also God
Death of Christ: He didn't die and rise again	**Death of Christ:** He died and rose again in the same body
Bible: Corrupted	**Bible:** Not sorrupted
Salvation: By faith plus works when good deeds outweigh bad ones	**Salvation:** Not by works but is a free gift of God for all who believe

HINDUISM	CHRISTIANITY
God: There are many gods (Polytheism). God is impersonal; Brahma is an abstract formless eternal being	**God:** There is one Theistic God (Theism). God is a spiritual being found in three Persons (Mathew 3:13–17; Book of 2 Corinthians 13:14)
Jesus: Jesus was one of a number of great holy men (but not perfect). It is an absurd idea that Jesus suffered on the cross. As a holy man, He was beyond pain and suffering.	**Jesus:** Jesus is the one and only Son of God. Jesus was crucified, suffered and died for our sins on the cross
Sin: Humanity's problem is "ignorance," not sin	**Sin:** Humanity is born with a sin nature and is in a state of moral "rebellion" agains God
Salvation: "Enlightenment brings a man from humanity to God and requires one's personal effort(s)	**Salvation:** There is only one way to salvation and it is through Jesus Christ (John 14:16)

Do you see the vast, unbridgeable differences between the core doctrines of each of these three major world religions? To say that all religions are the same and lead to the same place is to deny each religion its unique traditions; plus it violates the Law of Identity. So rather than being tolerant, pluralism is an intolerant view. By blending all religious beliefs, it denies each world religion its unique traditions and beliefs.

For example, a Muslim does not believe that Christ is God and that he died on the cross for the sins of all mankind. A Christian does not believe that Muhammad was a prophet, let alone the last prophet. A Hindu can only accept Jesus as a god among 300 million other gods; he cannot accept Jesus as the singular God of the universe. Religious pluralism is politically incorrect and offensive to people in all religions. While NAM attempts to redefine who Jesus Christ is and what he taught, the truth is evident: Jesus Christ is unique among all other gods.

CONCLUSION

It is essential that today's Christian be equipped to respond to the coexist mantra because we are the stewards of the Christian faith for our generation and generations yet to come. The greatest modern threat to orthodox Christianity is NAM's belief in relativism. Relativism is the belief that something can be true for you but not for me, or right for you but not for me. This view is fueled by New Age secular humanism, the belief that humankind is the ultimate ideal and that people are complete within themselves as the highest level of the evolutionary ladder and the measure of all things.[18]

Relative thinking leads to a relative view of biblical Christianity and Scripture. As a result, even some Christians buy into the false belief that all religions can lead to the same spiritual truth. This defies logic. All religions cannot be true because they teach opposite things as true. As mentioned in chapter one, the Law of Noncontradiction states that two systems of religious thought cannot be the same. If they were same, they would not be two different religions.

The Law of Identity says an object is the same as itself. If it were not, then it would not be itself. We cannot say, for example, that a tiger, a dog, and an alligator are all elephants. Each animal has its own identity. If each had the same identity, there would be no differences between the three. The same can be said of religion. We cannot say that Christianity, Islam, and Hinduism are all the same because they all make different truth claims. If all religions led to the same place, it would be mandatory that their core theological doctrines have the same identities, and they do not—not by any reasonable measure. Pluralism, therefore, is self-defeating because it fails to keep its identity; instead, it melds contradictory identities. (See chapter one on worldviews.)

This takes us back to my friend Cheryl who asserted that it is arrogant to think that Christ is the *only* way to heaven. Like Cheryl, many people choose to be willfully blind because we do not want to be convicted by the absolute truth about the reality of God.[19] A rejection of absolute truth leads to religious pluralism. If you are a Christian, you believe the Bible and what Jesus says about truth and God. Therefore, you cannot accept religious pluralism as a valid belief system.

Jesus claimed to be the truth. He said, *"I am the way and the truth and the life. No one comes to the Father except through me"* (John 14:6). Jesus also said, *"Anyone who does not enter the sheep pen by the gate, but climbs in by some other way, is a thief and a robber . . . I am the gate; whoever enters through me will be saved"* (John 10:1, 9).

Jesus' disciples affirmed his claims. For example, Peter said, *"Salvation is found in no one else, for there is no other name under heaven given to mankind by which we must be saved"* (Acts 4:12). And in 1 Timothy 2:5, the apostle Paul wrote, *For there is one God and one mediator between God and mankind, the man Christ Jesus.*

Sincerity is not a test for truth, and any of us can be sincerely wrong (Proverbs 14:12). Remember the *Titanic*? The craftsmen of the ship sincerely thought it was unsinkable, but it was not. Those who seek the true light will find it. *God shows no partiality, but in every nation anyone who fears him and does what is right is acceptable to him* (Acts 10:34–35 ESV). *And without faith it is impossible to please God, because anyone who comes to him must believe that he exists and that he rewards those who earnestly seek him* (Hebrews 11:6).[20]

A religious pluralist would say, "Your religion is true for you, but mine is true for me," thus claiming that religious truth is subjective. But the claim that religious truth is subjective is itself an objective truth claim.

If even one of those blind men who touched the elephant had his vision restored to see the truth, then he would look at what he was touching and see it was an elephant. At that point, would he not be able to show the rest of the men that they were wrong by having them examine the whole elephant? The truth is absolute: It was an elephant.

And the truth about Jesus is also absolute: while there are many ways to Jesus, Jesus is the only way to God. Being equipped to reach the lost for Christ in our multicultural world, whether in the marketplace or at the university, mandates the ability to show that Jesus is unique among all others who claimed to be God. One of the key ways to do that is to prove that Jesus did, beyond a reasonable doubt, rise from the dead. That is the focus of the next chapter.

CHAPTER 4

DID JESUS REALLY RISE FROM THE DEAD?

By J. Thomas Bridges, PhD

And if Christ has not been raised, your faith is futile; you are still in your sins. —1 Corinthians 15:17

An alternate title for this chapter could have been "Is it reasonable to believe that Christ's resurrection is a historical fact?" This is probably more precise, but it does not make for as catchy a chapter title. This chapter will explore the question (as it is alternately stated), and in order to do justice to answering such a question, we will approach it in phases. We have sketched out a case where we will first look at preliminary issues. These are issues that deal with the "reasonable" part of the question and address what would push an individual one way or the other in answering yes or no. Next, we will look at the main arguments for a yes response. As with any chapter, this one can either be either comprehensive or concise, but it cannot be both. We will not deal with all the preliminary issues, arguments, or objections. What this chapter is intended to do is to introduce you to these areas, give you some things to think on, and point you to further resources on this topic.

PRELIMINARY ISSUES

The Existence of God and Possibility of Miracles

The first of the preliminary issues, since it reaches the broadest scope, is whether or not miracles are possible. The reason this is a preliminary issue is that the belief that Jesus rose from the dead is a belief that a particular miracle, the resurrection, happened. If miracles are not possible, however, then this particular miracle is also not possible, and other considerations are moot. We will define *miracle* as "an event that has solely God as its cause." This is an important distinction because oftentimes *miracle* is defined as "a rare event." This latter definition would allow any number of highly improbable but wholly natural events to count as miracles. Our definition avoids this problem and sets the boundaries of what can and cannot count among the miraculous. Note, given this definition of what a miraculous event is, by definition, it requires God to exist. We are not arguing that miracles happen; therefore, God exists. We are simply pointing out the obvious fact that if a miracle is an event that has solely God as its cause, then belief in miracles entails a belief that God exists. If one does not believe God exists, then one will not believe in the possibility of miracles.

The broader question touching on the resurrection—are miracles possible?—therefore demands us to answer a previous question: does God exist? This question has been addressed in chapter two, but we raise it again here because the belief in or rejection of God's existence does play a role in how we judge historical evidence for events claimed to be miraculous. William Lane Craig summarizes this point nicely:

> *Naturalism, in contrast to supernaturalism, holds that every effect in the world is brought about by causes that are themselves part of the natural order (the space-time world of matter and energy). ... [When] inferring to the best explanation, one chooses from a pool of live options a candidate that serves as the best explanation of the evidence. For the naturalistic New Testament critic confronted with evidence concerning the empty tomb, the hypothesis that Jesus rose from the dead would not even be a live option.*[1]

So if one answers the question of God's existence with no, then there is no further reason to believe that Jesus rose from the dead. Though it is possible that an individual, on examining the historical evidence for Jesus' resurrection, might come to believe both that God exists and that he raised Jesus from the dead simultaneously. It is still the case, however, that there is a logical priority of the existence of God, and this typically plays a significant role in how one weighs the historical evidence.

THE OBJECTIVITY OF HISTORY

We will not linger over the question of whether historical events can be known as objective facts, but it is a preliminary issue to the resurrection. Later in this chapter, we will see historical testimony brought forward as evidence for this unique and central claim of Christianity. If historical testimony is hopelessly subjective or rationally unacceptable on other grounds, then this testimony cannot possibly give us reasons to believe in the resurrection. So the question is, can historical events be known with some objectivity?

There are some motivations for believing that history, or historical facts, cannot be objectively known. Some will object, for example, that the historian is faced with only fragmentary evidence for his historical thesis. What follows from this, the subjectivist will say, is that this historian must select, collate, and interpret his data and reproduce for his audience some account that is greater than the original data he had. Therefore, history is more created than objectively known.

Another objection that motivates a subjectivist view of history is that every historian is himself situated in a specific time and place. He is so removed from the times and places of the events on which he is commenting that he gives us an account seen only from his present perspective, or what some call historical conditioning. This means that what a twenty-first-century historian might say about events in first-century Palestine is hopelessly littered with his own interpretive framework, which is largely informed by his own historical situation.

Author and theologian Norman Geisler offers some concise responses to the above objections to the objectivity of history:

> *If by objective the subjectivists mean absolute knowledge, then of course no human historian can be objective. On the other hand, if objective means an accurate and adequate presentation that reasonable people should accept, then the door is open to the possibility of objectivity.... Objectivity resides in the view that best fits all the facts into the overall system; that is, into systematic consistency.*[2]

Responding to the objection from the historian's situatedness, Geisler writes:

> *It is true that every historian is a product of his time; each person does occupy a relative place in the changing events of the spatio-temporal world. However, it does not follow that because the historian is a product of his time, his history is also purely a product of the time. That a person cannot avoid a relative place in history does not mean his perspective cannot attain a meaningful degree of objectivity. This criticism confuses the content of knowledge and the process attaining it. ... Further, if relativity is unavoidable, then the position of the historical relativist is self-refuting, for either their view is historically conditioned and therefore unobjective, or else it is not relative but objective.*[3]

A final observation should suffice to bring this section to a close. Geisler also notes that "the very fact that one can know that some histories are better than others reveals that there must be some objective understanding of the events by which this judgment is made."[4]

As is true of all other versions of thoroughgoing relativism, historical relativism ends up being self-defeating. Geisler's observation is most telling. The fact that we can look at two historical accounts and judge one of them objectively better than the other means that there are some facts of the matter, as well as a grasp of the psychological and sociological issues surrounding the events, that make a particular historical account reasonably objective—not known with absolute certainty but known with a degree of reasonability. This is all we need to preserve the possibility of objective historical evidence for a purportedly miraculous event.

THE INTEGRITY OF THE GOSPELS

This is an important preliminary issue, as well as being an apologetics issue worthy of book-length treatment. Here we can only briefly address the ideas of whether or not the New Testament documents (specifically the gospels) are reliable regarding their (1) authorship and (2) contents. If the authorship of the documents is questionable or the content has been horribly corrupted, then the testimonies of the New Testament writers about the resurrection are not reliable evidence. In recent years, some critical New Testament scholars, such as Bart Ehrman, have deemed the New Testament documents unreliable for elucidating historical facts because they are corrupted and of later authorship. But as is true of nearly every area of scholarship, where there is a liberal reading of the data, there is also a conservative reading. We will look at a conservative reading of the data and offer some justification for this reading.

New Testament documents scholar Craig Blomberg gives us insight into the authorship of, specifically, the gospels and the book of Acts. The following is a somewhat lengthy quotation that gives a wonderful summary of the issue. Blomberg writes:

> *Modern biblical criticism has made two different kinds of claims about the authorship of the gospels and Acts. On the one hand, it has rightly pointed out that these five books are, strictly speaking, anonymous. None of the gospels or the book of Acts originally had a writer's name*

> *attached to it. Titles (for example, "The Gospel according to . . .") were likely added early in the second century when the fourfold gospel collection circulated as a unit. On the other hand, modern scholarship has more speculatively also questioned the accuracy of the traditional ascriptions of the authorship of these books to Matthew, Mark, Luke, and John. There are no dissenting traditions whatever in the first centuries of the Church's history concerning the authorship of the first three gospels and Acts and concerning the repeated claims that these books were indeed written by Matthew, Mark, and Luke. Given that two of these men were not apostles (Mark and Luke), and that Matthew would have been one of the most "suspect" of the apostles, in light of his background as a tax collector, it seems unlikely that the first Christians would have invented these authorship claims if they were merely trying to enhance the credibility of the documents attributed to these writers. Later apocryphal gospels and acts are consistently attributed to less suspect writers—for example, Peter, James . . . even Mary. There is some uncertainty in the early centuries about the Gospel of John, but it surrounds which "John" was behind the fourth gospel (John the apostle or a later John the elder), not whether or not the book was written by someone named John. And the clear majority opts for the apostle.*[5]

The most telling observation that Blomberg offers, besides the historical data of the early church's witness to the authorship of the texts, is that later apocryphal works, like the Gospel of Peter, attribute authorship of the writing to the well-known leader of the early church. This is in stark contrast to the strong tradition that attributes the synoptic gospels to Matthew (a tax collector and relatively minor figure in the early church), Mark (not an apostle), and Luke (also not an apostle). The tradition is that Mark and Luke are reliable because Mark wrote down what he heard from Peter (an eyewitness) and Luke investigated among the early believers for the eyewitness source material of his gospel account.

The fact that the early writings were anonymous can be likened to the fact that some small towns do not have street signs. Why? The community is so small and the terrain so familiar that no one needs to name the streets to know where everything is. In a similar way, the early church was small enough and the copies of authoritative writings so apparent in their source that they did not need to place names on them. Only later, as Blomberg says, when the gospels were collected as a unit did it become necessary to distinguish them by their authorship. The idea of the authors of the gospels being eyewitnesses or derivative of eyewitness accounts is directly related to the manuscript evidence for the text itself. After all, an eyewitness account is not much good if its contents have been radically corrupted. But it is important also to note an observation by New Testament scholar Gary Habermas: "Even though he says he would argue for the traditional gospel authors, R. T. France makes the point that it is not essential whether their identity is known. These books should be judged the way most historians judge historical accuracy—by their early date and the tradition behind them."[6] So, even though the tradition is strong identifying the gospel authors, the crucial historical question is, have the accounts themselves been radically corrupted or have they been well preserved?

The question of assessing the reliability of the New Testament documents must fall under the broader heading of this question: How does one assess the reliability of ancient documents? We want to ask this question because it would be unfairly biased to submit the New Testament documents to rigors that far exceed those of other ancient documents. After all, the question here is not whether the original authors were truly inspired by God to pen what they did. Rather, the question is, are these documents, as ancient documents, reliable in terms of their authorship and contents, leaving aside theological considerations?

Well-known scholar, the late F.F. Bruce, helps us in this regard. He provides a glimpse into the world of Ancient Near Eastern (ANE) documents and the manuscript evidence on which rests their reliability. He writes:

> *For Cæsar's Gallic War (composed between 58 and 50 BC), there are several extant MSS [manuscripts], but only nine or ten are good, and*

the oldest is some 900 years later than Cæsar's day.... The History of Thucydides (c. 460–400 BC) is known to us from eight MSS, the earliest belonging to c. AD 900. ... The same is true of the History of Herodotus (c. 488–428). Yet no classical scholar would listen to an argument that the authenticity of Herodotus or Thucydides is in doubt because the earliest MSS of their works which are of any use to us are over 1,300 years later than the originals.[7]

Bruce has given us a small picture of what it is like to test the reliability of ancient manuscripts. Greek scholar Bruce Metzger offers his own comparison:

In evaluating the significance of [the] statistics of the amount of Greek evidence for the text of the New Testament, one should consider, by way of contrast, the number of manuscripts which preserve the text of the ancient classics. Homer's Iliad, for example, the 'bible' of the ancient Greeks, is preserved in 457 papyri, 2 uncial manuscripts, and 188 miniscule manuscripts.... The works of several ancient authors are preserved to us by the thinnest possible thread of transmission.... In contrast with these figures, the textual critic of the New Testament is embarrassed by the wealth of his material.... Instead of the lapse of a millennium or more, as is the case of not a few classical authors, several papyrus manuscripts of portions of the New Testament are extant which were copied within a century or so after the composition of the original documents.[8]

What Bruce and Metzger have given us is an incomplete but very telling contrast between the typical amounts of available material for a textual scholar and the typical gaps for ancient documents between the writing of the original and extant copies. These are important facts if one is going to grasp the relative strength of the documentation for the text of the New Testament.

Metzger further expounds on the sources available for getting back to the content of the original manuscripts. He says, "Three classes of witnesses are available for ascertaining the text of the New Testament; they are the Greek manuscripts, the ancient translations into other languages, and the quotations from the New Testament made by early ecclesiastical writers."[9] This latter point is important because not only do we have copies of New Testament documents in the original Greek (over 5,000), but we also have the contents of the originals from copies translated to other languages (e.g. Coptic and Latin), and we have the contents quoted in the letters written by early church fathers.

F.F. Bruce notes, "Fortunately, if the great number of MSS increases the number of scribal errors, it increases proportionately the means of correcting such errors, so that the margin of doubt left in the process of recovering the exact original wording is not so large as might be feared; it is in truth remarkably small."[10] By comparing the overwhelming number of documents, even if there are errors in every single one, the same error will not be repeated in every one. There will, consequently, be evidence from the manuscripts as to which variant is likely the original reading. This gives us reasonably high confidence that the content of the New Testament documents that we have in our modern Bible does not differ significantly from the words of the original authors.[11]

SOME EVIDENCE FOR THE RESURRECTION

As has been noted throughout the chapter, the purpose here is to give the reader a sketch of the issues surrounding one's belief that Jesus in fact rose from the dead. So far we have touched on the preliminary issues of the possibility of miracles, the objectivity of history, and the integrity of the New Testament documents. We have finally come to the point of examining some of the evidence that makes the resurrection a reasonable historical fact. There are many book-length treatments of the myriad of evidences along with detailed analyses of the thesis for and against each point related to the historicity of the resurrection. Here we have selected a handful of evidences, either because they are the more common reference or because we find them particularly persuasive. What follows is in no way an exhaustive treatment.

Gary Habermas provides a list of the elements in the gospel accounts that represent an overwhelming consensus among scholars on the historical Jesus. That is, virtually every historical fact on this is considered largely undisputed by the men and women who study the historical evidence professionally. Of the dozen historical facts, I'll list eight, retaining their original numeration:

1) Jesus died by Roman crucifixion.
2) He was buried, most likely in a private tomb.
3) Jesus' tomb was found empty soon after his interment.
4) The disciples had experiences they believed were actual appearances of the risen Jesus.
5) Due to these experiences, the disciples' lives were thoroughly transformed.
6) The proclamation of the resurrection took place early, at the beginning of church history.
7) The disciples' public testimony and preaching of the resurrection took place in the city of Jerusalem, where Jesus had been crucified and buried shortly before.[12]

Individually or collectively, this list of historical facts is insufficient to prove that Jesus died and rose again from the dead. The resurrection of Jesus as an actual historical event is what William Lane Craig referred to early as the "best explanation" of the facts we have at hand. What history gives evidence of is that Jesus was actually killed (i.e. his death was not faked) and days after his confirmed execution, he was seen again by his disciples. Why believe this is the best explanation? This is where subsequent lines of evidence come along to support the resurrection as the best explanation. At this point, we will begin selecting the elements of that vast sea of data that are to us most provocative.

The first element that is most compelling is the fact that the earliest recorded testimony for Jesus' resurrection is sourced from a group of mildly hysterical women. At the beginning of the twenty-first century in the Western world, we live in an age that highly values egalitarianism (the equal rights of men and women), but for most of human history and in many cultures, this was not the case. In first-century Palestine, as in most times and places, women did not have the same rights as men. Women could not own property, which meant that a daughter could not inherit her father's estate (a factor motivating the plot in *Pride and Prejudice*). And more significantly related to the present issue, women could not give public testimony. That is, their testimony had zero weight under the law. This strikes me as having a distinct ring of truth. After all, the most ardent skeptic to the truth of Christianity would admit that if the disciples were doing anything in writing down the accounts of Christ's life and ministry, they were trying to persuade others to join their religion/community of belief. It would be unexplainable as to why the gospel writers would invent women as the earliest source about Christ's returning from death.

A second element or piece of evidence we find highly compelling is a combination of Habermas's facts #6, # 7, and # 8 from the above list. Namely, the disciples proclaimed this resurrection event (1) shortly after it happened, (2) among the persons who would have been most aware of and able to verify it, and (3) their lives were radically transformed. In other settings, Habermas reminded audiences that though the gospel accounts tell us about the life of Christ, which occurred chronologically before the events of the early church, the gospels themselves were written later than most of the New Testament documents; from the mid-AD 60s (for Mark) to the mid-AD 70s (for Matthew and Luke) to the mid-AD 90s (for John). Remember, most of the New Testament documents are letters that Paul, Peter, and John wrote to various churches or groups. In these writings (e.g. 1 Corinthians and Galatians), we get a glimpse into what the church believed within the first few decades of its founding. In terms of evidence for a particular belief in the ancient world, this is incredibly early.

Another enormously important fact is that the disciples advocated the resurrection event within the same city in which the event purportedly took place. In contrast to, say, proclaiming in Egypt or Rome or Persia that an obscure Jewish rabbi died and rose again. Some religions, e.g. Mormonism or Islam, are based on an account of an individual that is in no way verifiable. An individual has a private, purportedly supernatural experience and asks a community of individuals to believe their account on blind faith. With the disciples, however, we have a group of men and women all testifying publicly about an event whose elements are open to investigation and verification among those who (1) knew about the events surrounding it and (2) were in a position to immediately investigate the claims.

In the interest of philosophy, we have to digress a bit and address the nature of belief based on testimony. One may be skeptical about this or that report, or this or that source of a report, but one cannot adopt wholesale skepticism about believing based on the testimony of another. The reason is simple: most of what we know is based on the testimony of what we believe to be a credible witness/authority. If I were to ask you "how far away is the nearest large spiral galaxy to the Milky Way galaxy?" you would probably pull out your phone, Google it, open one of the more reputable astronomy sites, and tell me "the Andromeda Galaxy." And you would be correct. But how do you know that and why are you so confident about the belief? The answer is that if you go to a site run by NASA or an online magazine called *Universe Today*, you can be reasonably sure that the answer you get will not be a hoax or the information deliberately falsified. So the issue is, do you think the early gospel accounts are a hoax or their information deliberately falsified?

This is why Habermas's list is so important. It is a list of agreed upon historical events or elements related to the resurrection. Is it plausible that the disciples were trying to deceive people and included the testimony of women in their account given the social trends of the day? Is it plausible that the disciples were willfully propagating a hoax when they gave early public testimony among those who would be most familiar with their story and most able to verify its claims? It is certainly possible, but we do not believe it is a reasonable response.

This brings us to the last element from Habermas's list that we find compelling, and that is the way the resurrection event changed the lives of the disciples. It is not that they were willing to die for their beliefs and that none of them recanted their testimony on pain of torture, death, or exile. We know that many defenders of the resurrection point to these facts, and certainly they are consistent with the disciples wholeheartedly believing their testimony about Christ, but what we find compelling is a bit more primitive than all this. Let's elaborate.

When we watch a movie, the thing that is most concerning to us is the development of the characters. Is the main character changed by what he experiences, and in what ways is he changed? Are those changes psychologically plausible? For example, in one particular movie, one of the main characters says she was abandoned by her father at an early age and could care less where he is or what has happened to him. Just a few minutes later, when another character finds out her father was involved in some sort of black-market dealings that ultimately led to his murder, her response is "I'm coming with you because I want to know what happened to my father." It was obviously a reaction calculated to move the plot along, but wholly contrary to the character as she had been previously presented.

This element of psychological plausibility is what gives fiction a sense of reality and what gives historical accounts their ring of truth. In this vein, what we find compelling in the disciples' reaction is that they seem genuinely shocked by the resurrection. We tend to have this image of ancient folks as slightly moronic or highly gullible perhaps. After all, these are the types of people who think thunder is related to the anger of the gods. We think that, but as early as the sixth century BC, there were natural philosophers (the earliest scientists) who were looking for natural explanations of natural events. These ancient people may not have understood how nature functioned in the ways that it did, but they were familiar with common vs. uncommon events. We see this in the disciples' reaction to, for example, Jesus walking on water in the midst of a storm. They are awed by his actions because whatever else they know about the world, they know that men do not walk on water.

In a similar way, the disciples' reaction to the resurrection strikes me as psychologically plausible. That is, they understood Jesus as a brilliant rabbi (with his unique explanations of the Mosaic law) or a miracle-working prophet (e.g. raising Lazarus from the dead or making the blind see), but when he is dragged off by the local Jewish authorities, placed on trial before the highest Roman official in the land, and handed over for flogging and execution, they realized he was subject to all the normal political and juridical powers of the day. Then came Sunday morning. The tomb is empty, the hysterical women speak of angels and seeing Jesus ... then Jesus appears. That can't be him; it must be his ghost; nope, not a ghost, he is eating with us. The disciples' reactions to Christ are exactly what we would expect from a real event—completely psychologically plausible.

Our final piece of evidence is directly related to the study of philosophy. In graduate school, students read the earliest Pre-Socratic philosophers (those before Socrates) and then work their way over several years through the history of Western philosophy. When you study the history of ideas, you can see how one thinker is influenced (either positively or negatively) by a tradition of thinking. For example, one can trace the influence of Immanuel Kant from the late eighteenth century, through the existentialism of the nineteenth century, and all the way to the work of some thinkers in the early twentieth century. Studying the history of ideas makes one more acutely aware of how ideas emerge and evolve over time.

The last element we find compelling about the resurrection is the unique idea among early Christians that a single individual rose from the dead, that this event was somehow a picture of our eventual resurrection, and that both of these have enormous theological importance. This is made clear by an article written by biblical scholar N.T. Wright. The blessedness of this article is that it utilizes about fourteen pages in Wright's summary of his 700-page book, *The Resurrection of the Son of God*. The intriguing issue in this article is Wright's demonstration that the

Christian idea of the resurrection is absolutely unique. He writes:

> *One of the things I really enjoyed when I wrote that book [The Resurrection of the Son of God] was going back to my classical stomping grounds and researching ancient beliefs about life after death, Greek and Roman and Egyptian beliefs about life after death. And there's a huge range of beliefs, but "resurrection" doesn't feature in the Greco-Roman world.... We can track the way in which resurrection belief occurs in Judaism. Resurrection is a two-stage sequence: right after you die you're immediately in this holding pattern or waiting state; and then you have this entirely new life called resurrection.... The Pharisees believed in resurrection, and this seems to have been the majority belief in Palestinian Judaism at the time of Jesus. The Sadducees didn't believe in life after death at all, certainly not resurrection. And people like Philo and perhaps the Essenes (though that's controversial) believed in a single-stage disembodied immortality, in which, after death, you simply go wherever you are going and stay there.*[13]

Wright has done us the service of painstakingly comparing the idea of a personal resurrection among four different cultures (Egyptian, Roman, Greek, and Jewish), then looking deeper into the Jewish tradition on the subject.

The question to keep in mind here is this: Is there any history of ideas or previous conception of the resurrection that would have reasonably influenced the ideas of the early church? Wright gives seven unique distinctions about the early Christian view of resurrection. We'll include below the most interesting:

> *First, instead of resurrection being something that was simply going to happen to all God's people at the end, the early Christian said it had happened to one person in advance. Now, no first-century Jew, as far as we know, believed there would be one person raised ahead of everybody else.... Second, they believed that the resurrection would involve the transformation of the physical body. Those Jews who believed in resurrection seem to have gone in one of two directions. Some said it would*

> *produce a physical body exactly like this one all over again, and others said it would be a luminous body, one shining like a star. The early Christians didn't say either of those things. They talked about a new sort of physicality...that picture of the resurrection is not in Judaism.*
>
> *Second, and finally, we find that in early Christianity there is virtually no spectrum of belief about what happens after death. In Judaism there were several different viewpoints, and in the pagan world there were a great many, but in early Christianity there was only one: resurrection itself.... All this forces us as historians to ask a very simple question: Why did all the early Christians known to us, from the earliest times for which we have evidence, have this very new, but remarkably unanimous, view of resurrection?*[14]

These observations are interesting for several reasons. The entire community of early Christians (for about the first twenty years) were Jewish. That means that their religious views are largely Jewish in nature. Witness the early debates over whether or not Gentile believers were required to be circumcised or follow the Mosaic law. Also, in the history of Christianity, there is a trend toward widespread theological debate as the well-trained and the intelligent of the church attempt to understand the meaning of a particular doctrine (e.g. the incarnation). If Wright is correct with his final point, there was no such widespread debate leading to a spectrum of beliefs about the nature of the resurrection. The unanimity of the early church on this topic is eerie, to say the least.

What is the best explanation of this novel view of the resurrection being suddenly introduced into Jewish culture by a group of largely unschooled men and women and then held unanimously by the early church? The historical fact of Jesus' resurrection seems reasonable. Further, it explains the nature of the apostle Paul's subsequent ministry. Something so novel and yet Messianic and supernatural had happened that it required the Jews to understand its ramifications on their traditional views of Judaism. This would not have been the case if the early Christian's view of the resurrection had a substantial root in previous Judaic traditions.

CONCLUSION

The modification of our original question was, is it reasonable to believe that Christ's resurrection is a historical fact? We looked at preliminary issues related to the possibility of miracles, the objectivity of history, the integrity of the New Testament text, and finally looked at what we considered the most compelling lines of evidence that Jesus' resurrection can be reasonably believed to be a historical fact. Of course, there are those who object to nearly every one of the above points. Some believe that God cannot possibly exist, and therefore miracles are not possible. Some think that history is too subjective to give us historical fact. Others think that history as history is incapable of attesting to a miraculous event. Some who are aware of even more available evidences than those sketched above remain unconvinced. But the question was not, is the evidence so overwhelming that even one who wants to be skeptical simply cannot be? The question was, is belief in the resurrection as a historical fact r*easonable*. That is, is it possible for one to have a scholarly understanding of all the relevant historical data and conclude that Jesus did in fact rise from the dead? The answer to that question is yes; it is perfectly reasonable. Many highly educated, scholarly individuals are persuaded that a balanced view (not a biased view) of the historical evidence leans heavily in favor of the resurrection as the best explanation of all the relevant historical facts. The Christian need have no fear that this central belief is somehow based on blind faith or without any evidential support.

① Did God create evil.
If God created evil and evil is something, didn't God create evil?
No, He created our ability to have free will which made way for evil.
◦ God created ONLY good things

Where does moral evil come from +
Why didn't He make perfect human beings that cannot be corrupted?
• 1st Satan's fall
2nd in the garden
Traditional Answer is – "Free Will"
= our ability to make choices w/o external coercion
• Why doesn't an all good + all powerful God just stop the moral evil that's possible

God did this so

Heb 6:18
Free will disallows for NO free will.
Is it possible to destroy moral evil w/out destroying our present world + our freedom
The only way God could destroy evil is to destroy free will.
Humans don't choose devastating natural disasters – it's a byproduct of a good process.

1– what is evil

In suffering, PRAY. And, Know you are not alone.
Pray that God will take me through it, and not that God will take it from me.

Keep trusting God in the darkness
Trust God's heart.

Robert Jeffress

Faith—believing that God is going to overcome evil

Chapter 5

WHY DOES GOD ALLOW BAD THINGS TO HAPPEN TO GOOD PEOPLE?

If God were to eradicate all evil from this planet, he would have to eradicate all evil men. Who would be exempt? 'For all have sinned and fall short of the glory of God' *(Romans 3:23). God would rather transform the evil man than eradicate him.*[1] —Billy Graham

As a child, Ted Turner, founder of the CNN news media cable channel, dreamed of being a Christian missionary. But that changed when Turner's younger sister, Mary Jean, was diagnosed with a rare form of lupus, a disease that caused her to suffer a slow, painful death. After watching his sister experience such suffering, Turner rejected his Christian worldview and belief in God.

In an interview with Ann O'Neill of CNN on November 17, 2013, Turner stated, "She [Mary Jean] was sick for five years before she passed away. And it just seemed so unfair, because she hadn't done anything wrong. What had she done wrong? And I couldn't get any answers. Christianity couldn't give me any answers to that. So my faith got shaken somewhat."[2] After fifteen-year-old Mary Jean died, Turner's father killed himself. Turner then renounced religion altogether and embraced atheism: "If that's the type of God he is, I want nothing to do with him." By the mid 1980s, Turner developed serious mental problems. A psychiatrist diagnosed him with manic depression and put him on lithium.[3]

How we process pain in our lives and how suffering in the lives of others affects us are directly related to our worldview and faith in God. I am saddened when I think about the huge impact Ted Turner could have had for Christianity. Instead, pain and suffering led him to reject his Christian faith because nobody was able to provide him the answers to some difficult questions: If God is all good and all powerful, how could he allow Mary Jean to suffer so badly and die? Why would God allow such a terrible disease to destroy her? Human disease is a deprivation of good health, and evil is a lack of goodness. Hence, this terrible disease is evil.

HOW CAN AN ALL-GOOD GOD ALLOW EVIL?

One of the greatest perceived objectives or obstacles for people coming to trust in Jesus Christ as Lord and Savior is the problem of evil—trying to make sense of why bad things happen to good people. When we call ourselves "good," we do so in an allegorical sense because only God is good. In the biblical Scriptures, when a man called Jesus "good teacher," Jesus gave an interesting response: *"Why do you call me good?"* Jesus answered. *"No one is good—except God alone"* (Mark 10:18).

When we address the problem of why bad things happen to good people, it would be more appropriate to frame the discussion around bad things happening to people who were not engaging in some kind of risky behavior: for example, a non-smoker gets lung cancer or a careful, law-abiding driver gets hit by a drunk driver.

We cannot always look at an instance where evil has been allowed to affect us and then pinpoint a specific reason that particular bad thing was allowed to happen. However, in some cases, we are able to see God's providential hand in the rearview mirror of life. Have you ever looked back on something that you really wanted and prayed for, only to be thankful later that God did not answer your prayer according to what you wanted, but according to his will? In our quest to better understand why pain and suffering are allowed in the first place, let's look at what evil *is* and what it *is not*.

WHAT EVIL IS NOT

What does it mean for something or someone to be evil? Is evil a force or a lack of something (i.e. goodness)? A good place to start talking about what evil *is*, is to define what is *not*. Contrary to popular belief, evil is not a force, substance, or thing. Evil is not anything independent in and of itself. Many people believe that evil is literally the devil or that the devil is pure evil. But the devil cannot be pure evil because God created him. Outside of being created by God, the devil (Satan) is evil.[4] But what exactly is evil?

WHAT EVIL IS

Evil is a privation of good substances but not a real substance in and of itself, because a 100 percent privation leaves nothing of the original substance. In truth, evil is the *lack* of something—God's goodness. Because evil is not a substance, but the lack thereof, it is impossible for pure evil to exist as an independent entity.

Evil is like rot to a tree or rust to a car. If a car were 100 percent rusted out, it would no longer be a car. Likewise, if a tree is completely rotted, it is no longer a tree; it is dirt. Evil is a privation or corruption of the Creator's intended perfect, all-good creation. For example, the automobile maker (intelligent designer) did not design the car (intelligent design) to rust. Rust is a corruption of the perfect design intended by the original intelligent designer. The intelligent designer created the car to be without rust; thus rust is a privation and a corruption of that original design. In that sense, rust is evil.

In this way, evil exists on something else other than itself, but not in itself. For example, the moth holes in a garment could not exist without the garment. Likewise, evil cannot exist within any living being that has no sense of goodness.

Evil cannot exist in and of itself as a separate, independent entity because it is merely a privation of something good that is supposed to be there.[5] The fact that a stone cannot see because it has no eyes seems to challenge the claim of privation in relation to evil. In reality, there is no privation, but a mere absence of something (eyes) according to the design of a stone. In other words, stones were created or designed without eyes. This is very different than a man born blind, because functioning eyes are part of man's design. Blindness is a deprivation of sight, and thus blindness is a privation for a man but not for a rock.

While the man born blind has to endure sightlessness, which is an evil, that evil is not a condition of the man's own sinful or evil actions. The evil of blindness stems from original sin, birthed in Adam and Eve in the Garden of Eden, as stated in the book of Genesis chapter three.

Genesis 2:9 shows us that while God created a perfect world with perfect creatures, he also gave human beings free will by which to choose good or evil. Adam and Eve decided to defy God and choose evil by eating the fruit God had forbidden them to eat. Notice that the free will choice is represented in the tree of knowledge of good and evil, symbolizing God's intended perfect will for mankind. God is the intelligent designer of a perfectly created creation with a perfect ethic of goodness and with a perfect, best way of achieving God's plan through free will. When Adam and Eve chose to eat the fruit of the tree in the middle of the garden that God told them not to eat from, they chose out of God's will and ethic, thus creating a lack of goodness in a perfectly created world. As a result, Adam and Eve introduced sin and evil into the mortal world by defying God's command.

While evil is a deprivation, it manifests itself in different categories or ways. Two of those ways include moral depravity and physical depravation. An example of *moral depravation* would be sexual perversity, such as cheating on one's spouse, falsifying taxes records, or lying. An example of *physical depravation* would be the lack of sight or a physical mutilation. There are also bad relations between things. A relationship that is filled with hate is evil, while one filled with love is good.[6]

There is also a difference between metaphysical and moral evil. By metaphysical, I am speaking to a reality beyond what is perceived by the senses. This is a philosophical concept relating to the fundamental nature of reality, being, and existence. For example, is Satan pure evil in his existence or his being? We addressed this earlier: Satan (the devil) cannot be pure evil because God created him, and only in that sense is Satan good. Outside of being created by God, Satan is evil. This is what is meant by metaphysical evil.

THE DIFFERENCE BETWEEN METAPHYSICAL AND MORAL EVIL

While total evil in a metaphysical sense is impossible, total evil in a moral sense is not impossible. For example, millions of people around the world die of starvation every year because their corrupt governments prevent the necessary food from reaching them. The problem is not a deprivation of available food but a pre-meditated moral depravation by government leaders who seek to control their citizens through the availability of necessities such as food, water, and heat. The problem of moral evil again circles back to individual or corporate free will. It is possible for a moral being to be totally depraved morally but not metaphysically. In this way, it is possible for evil to extend to every part of a person's being, but impossible for evil to destroy the person. If it were possible for evil to destroy a person's being, there would be no person left to do any evil. Furthermore, evil cannot exist by itself as only evil because there would be nothing to deprive. Once something like a tree has fully rotted, it is no longer a tree but dirt. While evil decreases good, it is impossible to totally destroy evil in our current state metaphysically speaking.[7]

But there is another major form of evil to address—natural evil. What about the deprivation of goodness through pain and suffering caused by natural disasters?

IS NATURAL EVIL A CORRUPTION IN NATURE?

Why does God allow devastating wildfires, tornados, hurricanes, floods, and tsunamis? Better yet, why is there natural evil in the first place? After all, humans don't choose devastating natural disasters out of free will. Natural evil in the form of things such as natural disasters are a by-product of a good process. On the *Muddling Toward Maturity* blog, writer, scholar, and public intellectual Dinesh D'Souza addresses the problem of natural disasters by drawing from the book *Rare Earth: Why Complex Life Is Uncommon in the Universe* by Peter Ward and Donald Brownlee:

> *While natural disasters occasionally wreak havoc, our planet needs plate tectonics to produce the biodiversity that enables complex life to flourish on earth. Without plate tectonics, earth's land would be submerged to a depth of several thousand feet. Fish might survive in such an environment, but not humans. Plate tectonics also help regulate the earth's climate, preventing the onset of scorching or freezing temperatures that would make mammalian life impossible. In sum, plate tectonics are a necessary prerequisite to human survival on the only planet known to sustain life.*[8]

In other words, earthquakes are a consequence of plate tectonic-movement from giant rock formation plates under the ground in order to release pressure and produce the biodiversity necessary to sustain life. When those tectonic movements occur under the ocean floor, they can create a tidal wave called a tsunami. The famous 2004 Indian Ocean earthquake—which produced a tsunami that took the lives of between 230,000–280,000 people in fourteen countries—was a good, natural event, but the by-product was evil in that so many people died. Occasionally, these processes that keep the world in order may hurt or kill people as an unintended natural by-product of a good process.[9]

In an article titled "Why We Need Earthquakes," published in *Christianity Today*, Dinesh D'Souza again illustrates this point:

> *Our planet requires oxygen and a warming sun and water in order for us to live here, and we appreciate this, even though we recognize that people can get sunstrokes and drown in the ocean. So, too it seems that plate tectonics are . . . a "central requirement for life" as we know it.*[10]

God created the universe, the earth, and all the weather that occurs within them. Natural disasters are just that—natural.

DID GOD CREATE EVIL?

A major obstacle for many in the secular world and for many in the church is this: If God created everything, did he create evil? The syllogistic argument that God created evil is as follows:

1) God created all things.
2) Evil is something.
3) Therefore, God created evil.

Our response to that argument is simple:

1) Evil is not a thing.
2) Evil is a corruption of a good thing.[11]

CAN GOD CREATE EVIL?

God created only good things; evil is not a thing, so God did not create evil. Those arguing against the existence of God will say something like this: If God is absolutely perfect, he cannot create anything imperfect. Furthermore, a perfect creature cannot do evil. Therefore, evil cannot arise in such a world. But evil did arise in this world. Hence, either God is absolutely perfect, God cannot create anything imperfect, or both statements are false. If the statements are both false, then God is not perfect, and God did not create a perfect creature.[12]

CAN A PERFECT CREATURE DO EVIL?

On the other hand, if God did create perfect creatures, then how can a perfect creature commit evil?

A RESPONSE TO HOW PERFECT CREATURES CAN DO EVIL:

1) God is absolutely perfect.
2) God cannot create anything imperfect.
3) And a perfect creature cannot do evil.[13]

Premise 3 states that a perfect creature cannot do evil. How can a perfect creature do evil? While God created only good things, one good thing God created was free will. Free will makes evil possible since: (a) free will is the power to do something other than good; and (b) to do other than good is to do evil. Hence, a perfect creature with free will can do evil. While God made evil *possible*—via free will, which is good—free creatures made evil *actual* (actually happen.).[14]

CONCLUSION

As a result of evil and the anger and hurt that grew out of it, Ted Turner not only rejected God but also set out to oppose Christianity and Jesus Christ. His dream of becoming a missionary as a young person was destroyed by the thought that God would *allow* evil to cause his little sister to suffer so painfully and eventually die. Turner had questions about evil, pain, and suffering that nobody in the Christian community had answers to. He could not figure out what his beloved sister had done so wrong to deserve five years of severe suffering before succumbing to death.

How many other Ted Turners are out there whose faith could grow or be sustained if more Christians could articulate answers about evil? The bottom line is that Turner did not get his questions about pain and suffering answered. What would the world be like today if Turner had become a missionary or had started CNN with Christian ethics, morality, and values?

Turner's questions are not much different from the ones each of us ask. It is important that we correctly understand and share with others the truth about why an all-good God allows evil to happen in the first place And it is vital to know that natural disasters, which are a form of evil, are allowed to happen in spite of the widespread pain and suffering they cause. It is also important for us to understand that God did not create evil and that it is impossible for God to create evil due to his all-good nature.

When suffering affects our lives or those we love, it is only human to ask questions. But by having answers to some of these questions, we develop a more mature Christian faith. We also gain the ability to share with other people the truth about suffering in its correct context. We can be the person who provides those answers. But having those questions is only part of the equation. When we, or those around us, are going through trials, it is often our heart that bears the brunt of the pressure put on our faith. While we cannot ignore the head, in times of pain and suffering, we often need to lead with the heart. In the next chapter, we will take this head knowledge of pain and suffering and apply it to ministering to others with our heart.

CHAPTER 6

HOW DO I EXPLAIN EVIL, PAIN, AND SUFFERING TO OTHERS?

Evil and suffering are real. ... They aren't an illusion, nor are they simply an absence of good. We are fallen creatures living in a fallen world that that has been corrupted by sin, and we all share in its brokenness. Most of all, we share in its tragic legacy of disease and death.[1] —Billy Graham

In 1970, a young Sicilian immigrant by the name of Mauro achieved the American Dream. He had worked hard to complete his college degree in electrical engineering and had recently been promoted to an upper management level position rating of G13 where he worked at the United States Department of the Navy in Washington, DC. One spring day before sunrise, Mauro rested peacefully next to his wife, Vita. Their sons—John (age 11), Gary (age 9), Steven (age 5)—and daughter, Gail (one week old), were also sleeping. Vita awoke to the sound of Mauro having a massive heart attack. My father (Mauro) passed away almost immediately.

I watched the Laurel Rescue Squad carry him on a stretcher past my bedroom doorway—the last memory I have of my father. In the ensuing years, my mother did an incredible job of raising four children on her own—a feat she says was accomplished only by the hand of God in her life and on our family. She raised four respectful, successful children who completed our parents' dream of receiving a college education. All of us have married, and we have children of our own, providing nine grandchildren for Mom to enjoy. Three of us completed our master's degree, and my oldest brother built a successful real-estate business after college. And yet in the midst of these blessings, the question still looms: why was my father taken so young, leaving four children to grow up without a dad?

Three years after my father died, my mother was diagnosed with leukemia. When she went to the National Institutes of Health (NIH) in Washington, DC, the priest came in and gave her last rights. He also told her to get her papers and family in order because she would pass away within six months. My father's brother, John Garofalo, drove down from New Jersey within forty-eight hours and took my mom straight to the Memorial Sloan Kettering Cancer Center in New York City. But no one among our relatives could take on four kids should my mother pass away, so the final plan was to divide us between at least two, maybe three, other families.

By God's grace, for six months while my mother was getting her cancer treatment in NYC, we had incredibly hospitable neighbors who took us in. My brothers, John and Gary, and I lived with three different neighborhood families within one street of each other in Montpelier, MD, for the next six months. My sister, Gail, was only three years old and not in school yet, so she lived with my grandparents in Brooklyn, NY, while my mother was in the hospital.

Again the questions arose: Why had our father been taken from us at such an early age? Why was my mother fighting with all her Sicilian might to stay alive so she could raise her children? Why do bad things happen to good people? Why did such bad things happen to us?

To make sense of these questions, I give the disclaimer that in many, if not most, cases we cannot understand or pinpoint why something bad happens in our life. This is the problem of evil in the world. And trusting the Lord above human understanding is the key to gaining the peace that surpasses all understanding during times of evil, pain, and suffering (Philippians 4:7). In this chapter, I will equip you to better understand why bad things are allowed to happen to good people. In turn, this understanding will help you work through your own loss, pain, and suffering as well as minister to those around you with the truth and love of God.

Before we go any further, I will make an important point. When someone is experiencing pain, suffering, or loss of some sort, the best thing you can do is let them know three crucial things:

- First, you love them.
- Second, you are praying for them.
- And third, you are there for them.

The theology and Scripture discussed in this chapter are most helpful if digested prior to a tragic event. They also can be helpful when people ask why pain and suffering have been allowed to enter their lives. If someone asks for a theological or philosophical answer outside of Scripture during a time of suffering, my advice is to discuss the issue truthfully, but saturate the truth with love and compassion. Always minister to the heart first and the head second.

CAN GOD BRING GOOD OUT OF EVIL?

Dr. Norman Geisler writes that God can bring good out of evil because he is all powerful and he is able to redeem good even from evil. For example, a drowning person may inspire an act of bravery in the person who rescues him. This is called the "greater good." While a tree reduced to sawdust can be used to manufacture papers, God in his providence is able to redeem much (if not all) good out of the evil by-products in this world.

God would not permit evil to exist in his world unless he was so almighty and so good that he could produce good out of the depriving evil.

God may not always redeem good out of every single evil by-product in our fallen world within the moral or physical realm, but he does work all things together for good in his overall, perfect eternal plan. Our will is often in conflict with his will. Because we cannot see the future as God does, we must trust him. We must accept that he sees the whole parade as opposed to only knowing about the next float to turn the corner. In the event of evil, sometimes we do not know *why* things turn out the way they do; other times we are able to see what God is doing in our lives. God is in control, and we are not God. Perhaps this is part of the answer.

When speaking to others about the problem of evil, it is wise to attempt to understand exactly whom we are speaking with. Is that person experiencing pain in his or her life, or is that person attempting to disprove the existence of God?[2] How we respond to people who ask about the problem of evil often depends on why they are asking the question to begin with. In all cases, it is just as important to discover why somebody is asking the question as it is to answer the question. And understanding why someone is asking the question is essential to effectively answering the problem of evil in the lives of others.

ADDRESSING THE PROBLEM OF SUFFERING AND EVIL

When the problem of evil is raised by your *atheist* friends, it would be safe to assume they do not believe in the Bible as the truth. The problem of evil is an emotional subject, which more often than not is tied to a tragedy in a person's life. For this reason, we need to be sensitive as to what that person may have experienced and what their present spiritual condition is. You may want to tell your friends that while God granted us free will, we human beings are responsible for making it "actual" in that we execute the sin in mind and body, making it happen.

Why did God grant us free will to begin with? C. S. Lewis provides the answer in his book *Mere Christianity*:

> *Why then, did God give them free will? Because free will, though it makes sin possible, is also the only thing that makes possible any love or goodness or joy worth having. A world of automata—of creatures that worked like machines—would hardly be worth creating. . . . Of course God knew what would happen if they used their freedom the wrong way: apparently he thought it worth the risk.*[3]

In other words, God wanted us to freely love him. A forced love is no love at all. If God created the best of all possible worlds, why didn't he just stop moral evil from happening in the first place? Why didn't God create a world where evil was not possible?

WHY DOESN'T GOD STOP MORAL EVIL?

Why doesn't an all-good and all-powerful God stop moral evil, such as murder and rape, before it happens? Can he really do all things? The answer is no, God cannot do all things; he can only do those things that are possible. For example, God cannot do things like create a rock too large for him to lift. Why? God cannot create something greater than himself, and it is impossible for anything to be greater than God in the first place. On a level that speaks more to us as mere mortals, it is impossible for God to lie. The Book of Hebrews tells us this:

> *People swear by someone greater than themselves, and the oath confirms what is said and puts an end to all argument. Because God wanted to make the unchanging nature of his purpose very clear to the heirs of what was promised, he confirmed it with an oath. God did this so that, by two unchangeable things in which it is impossible for God to lie, we who have fled to take hold of the hope set before us may be greatly encouraged.* (Hebrews 6:16–18)

Scripture is clear that God cannot lie. Furthermore, verse 17 tells us that God is unchanging in both his nature and the nature of his purpose according to his oath. If God says something or makes a promise, it is impossible for God to break his word. In other words, it is *impossible* for God to lie (v. 18).

Free will disallows for no free will, and it is impossible to destroy moral evil without destroying our present world because moral evil is a by-product of free will. That would be as much of a contradiction as creating a square circle, which is impossible, even for God. God cannot force us to freely make good choices, so the only way God could destroy evil and bad things from happening to us altogether would be to destroy our freedom altogether. But free will is what allows us to freely love God and other people without compulsion. Would you really want to live in a world with no free will?

Now that we have addressed *moral* evil, what about *natural* evil such as natural disasters? After all, nobody likes natural evil (except perhaps the owners of weather television channels, who profit financially from natural disasters). Many atheists, as well as those who are struggling with their faith, are quick to proclaim that the problem of evil is evidence against the existence of God. They do this by addressing the *nature* of evil. Their argument is as follows:

OBJECTION: IF GOD IS ALL GOOD, HE WOULD DEFEAT EVIL

1) If God is all good, he would defeat evil.
2) If God is all powerful, he could defeat evil.
3) But evil is not defeated.
4) Therefore no such God exists.

(Note: This conclusion is not logical, since evil might yet still be defeated in the future.)

RESPONSE:

1) If God is all good, he would defeat evil.
2) If God is all powerful, he could defeat evil.
3) But evil is not yet defeated.
4) Therefore, evil will one day be defeated.

The nature of a theistic God guarantees evil's defeat. God is all powerful and can do it. He is all good and wants to do it. Hence, he will do it.[4]

THE DEFEAT OF EVIL BY A SAVIOR WHO SUFFERED

The good news is that while the effects of evil are allowed to affect our mortal lives, the book of Colossians tells us that evil has been defeated for eternity.

> *When you were dead in your sins … God made you alive in Christ. He forgave us all our sins, having canceled the charge of our legal indebtedness, which stood against us and condemned us; he has taken it away, nailing it to the cross. And having disarmed the powers and authorities, he made a public spectacle of them, triumphing over them by the cross.* (Colossians 2:13–15)

Jesus in his human form experienced pain and suffering; therefore, he understands our trials, pain, and suffering. It is comforting to know that we have an awesome God who knows pain, suffering, death, and loss on a mortal level—a truth that greatly differentiates Christianity from any other religion. The book of Hebrews makes this abundantly clear:

> *Since the children have flesh and blood, he too shared in their humanity so that by his death he might break the power of him who holds the power of death—that is, the devil—and free those who all their lives were held in slavery by their fear of death.* (Hebrews 2:14–15)

The actual *defeat* of evil is explained with greater detail in the book of Revelation, chapter 19:11–15 and 21:1–4. Now that we have addressed what evil is and the eventual defeat of evil, let's look to the *hope* we have in God.

BE ENCOURAGED

In Isaiah 38, God healed King Hezekiah from his suffering. Although Hezekiah was spared from death, God did not deliver him *from* his trials but *through* his trials. Hezekiah said, *"Surely it was for my benefit that I suffered such anguish. In your love you kept me from the pit of destruction; you have put all my sins behind your back"* (Isaiah 38:17). Notice what King

Hezekiah did before God healed him: he prayed. *Hezekiah turned his face to the wall and prayed to the Lord* (Isaiah 38:2).

Only after the trials could Hezekiah see the suffering was beneficial (v. 17). As Paul noted, *And we know that in all things God works for the good of those who love him, who have been called according to his purpose* (Romans 8:28). This promise is only for those who love God, and in this context *good* means conformity to Christ (v. 29) not our immediate comfort. The Bible also tells us:

> *Consider it pure joy, my brothers and sisters, whenever you face trials of many kinds, because you know that the testing of your faith produces perseverance. Let perseverance finish its work so that you may be mature and complete, not lacking anything.* (James 1:2–4)

Achieving that mind-set is easier said than done, but nonetheless, God has said it, and therefore it is both true and possible. The difference between the person dependent on God and the independent person is apparent on their faces when a similar tragedy strikes both of them. Being dependent on God gives us supernatural strength unattainable by our independent human existence alone. So be encouraged. God will carry us through our trials, and these trials will also strengthen our faith.

THE BEST WORLD POSSIBLE

It is conceivable that this present evil world is the best possible means of attaining the best world achievable. Our current world is a place where some are saved and some are lost, where sin is defeated and the greater good is achieved. If it is necessary for God to achieve the greatest possible good, then permitting this evil world as a necessary precondition for achieving the highest good would be the best alternative. This world has not yet achieved the greatest good. But this present evil world is the best means of achieving the end of the greatest good, which could not be achieved without the presences of evil. It is necessary for an all-good God to accomplish the best end. It follows that an all-powerful God can in fact achieve an end that does not involve any contradiction such as an all-good and all-powerful God allowing evil. In fact, it is contradictory to force freedom and free choice to achieve a moral end. Therefore, it is conceivable that this present evil world is the best possible means to obtaining the best world possible: one where some are saved and some are lost, a world where sin is defeated and a greater good is achieved.[5]

It is not that God cannot eliminate evil (bad things from happening) but that one day God will defeat evil and eliminate pain and suffering by bringing an end to this earth and creating a new heaven and a new earth as described in Revelation chapters 21–22. The good news and our hope lies in that the new earth will be free from evil, pain, suffering, and death.

When my mother had cancer, she fought for her life. She also prayed to God for six months that he would spare her life and let her raise her four children. My two brothers and I were driven up to New York City almost every weekend to see my mother in the hospital when she was physically able to see us. Along with a bone marrow transplant, she was also under a new experimental chemotherapy treatment.

One Sunday night, after I returned to the Keatings' house, where I was living while my mother was in the hospital with cancer, I felt an overwhelming sense of pain, helplessness, and fear that my mother would pass away, leaving us children split up and orphaned. The feelings came out of nowhere. It seemed like a load of bricks had fallen on my back. I went into the bathroom, dropped to my knees, and prayed a simple prayer: "God, you took my father early. Please leave us mom so that we can be a family again and stay together."

The following Sunday, Mr. and Mrs. Keating told us there would be a special event happening that evening and that each of us had a special assignment. My job turned out to be the door greeter, which fit my personality. When the first guests arrived, I opened the door. Standing before me was my entire family. My mom's friend Ron held up my little sister Gail (whom I called my little buddy). When I saw my family, I said to myself, "This is the greatest day of my life."

In the ensuing months, Mrs. Keating led my mother into a relationship with Jesus Christ. My mother says she went to church with Mrs. Keating one day, where they laid hands on her and prayed over her. She was in remission from that day forward. She cannot explain it any better than to say that during the prayer, the pain and sickness from the chemotherapy went away—the hand of God on her life. Seventeen years later, Mrs. Keating's son, Michael, led me into a relationship with Jesus Christ by persuading me to attend a Bible study with him.

Why was all this suffering and pain allowed to fall on my family? Here is the way I see it: Yes, my father was taken from me so young. I also almost lost my mother and my siblings. But I did not. So I am grateful for what God gave our family not ungrateful for what he did not give us. Plenty of children have no parents or abusive parents. Along with my mom, brothers, and sister, I have been blessed and provided for beyond comprehension. In God's providence, he gave me a close-knit, supportive, extremely grateful, and loving family. To this day, my family members are there for one another.

While I have explained what the nature of evil is and why evil, suffering, and pain are permitted to affect our lives, I cannot offer you a silver bullet that will solve all the pain and suffering in life. What I have offered you is a biblical perspective that you can adopt in effort to better understand the pain and suffering that are part of life. All of us have experienced evil, pain, suffering, and loss. And at some point in the future, we will experience those things again. How we respond to such difficulties—whether we turn to God and Scripture or turn away from them—is the differentiating factor in who we become on this earth and in eternity. Bad things happen. No human being has ever been spared the effects of evil. It is not a matter of *if* but *when*. How wonderful to know that our hope can be put in the supernatural God of the universe, who has promised to carry us through the times when evil is permitted to affect our lives.

WHEN WE ARE UNABLE, THE HOLY SPIRIT IS ABLE

When you are too engulfed in pain or anger to pray clearly, remember that God did not leave us alone when Jesus was taken up in bodily form into heaven. He left us a helper, his Holy Spirit, to help us manage the effects of evil in the form of pain, suffering, and loss in our lives. Jesus promised, *"But the advocate, the Holy Spirit, whom the Father will send in my name, will teach you all things and will remind you of everything I said to you"* (John 14:26).

When I fell to my knees and asked God to spare my mother and began praying for God's help, I became unable to speak to God verbally because I was weeping too hard to form coherent words. Later, I learned that in such cases *the Spirit helps us in our weakness. We do not know what we ought to pray for, but the Spirit himself intercedes for us through wordless groans. And he who searches our hearts knows the mind of the Spirit, because the Spirit intercedes for God's people in accordance with the will of God* (Romans 8:26–27). God knows our heart and needs, and the Holy Spirit is always available to help us through the most difficult times.

TIMES OF PAIN AND SUFFERING MAKE US BETTER

When our friends, coworkers, and loved ones suffer, God often provides a window of opportunity to show his truth and love in those teachable moments. God uses the empathy and strength we have gained from our own trials to minister to others who are experiencing similar trials. But if we are not involved in their lives during those moments, we risk missing the blessing and window of opportunity the Lord has given us to minister to others.

Understanding the theology of suffering and what the Bible says about it is crucial to understanding why suffering, pain, and evil exist. Working through the pain in our lives, as well as comforting those around us, is much more effective when we gain this understanding prior to difficult times. The proper starting place is to be still and listen to God, study his Word, and spend time on our knees in prayer. As we develop those habits, the Spirit of God will comfort us and provide for us in ways that we cannot explain.

Our starting point when we minister to others during times of pain and suffering is a listening ear. Billy Graham offers wise advice about ministering to others who are suffering: "A suffering person does not need a lecture—he needs a listener."[6] To "be there" for someone may sound too simple, but availability often is the best way to help.

CONCLUSION

These chapters on evil were designed to give you hope and improve your understanding of the biblical perspective on trials, pain, and suffering. When pain and suffering enter your life, this is my prayer for you: May God keep you, may his light shine upon you, and may he bless and protect you. And may you allow him to carry you *through* the trials of life.

When my mother was being treated for cancer back in 1973, two cancer specialists cared for her. As far as I know, one was a Christian and the other was not. One doctor emphasized that the new chemotherapy was an incredible discovery that saved her life; he gave full credit to the chemicals and human understanding. The other doctor, who was a Christian, said something quite different: she should not be alive because if the cancer did not kill her, the chemotherapy should have. Why? The chemo she was taking was a new experimental treatment. As a result, she received three times the dose of chemicals that should have been administered, which should have killed her. That doctor credited my mom's remission to the hand of God on her life. While God used the chemo treatment, it was ultimately God who spared my mom's life and cured her. Can we explain that? Not really. But my mother, brothers, sister, and I are all immeasurably thankful and indebted to God for sparing my mother's life and allowing us to grow older together as a family.

God is in control, and it is wise for us to trust him even when things seem out of control. Evil is real. It is a deprivation that we all have to deal with in our lives and in the lives of others. The next time you face trials and pain, pray that God will take you *through* not *from* those trials and suffering. And remember, when we see others suffering, the best thing we can do is "be there."

We place our hope in the God who is in control, in the God who will eliminate evil altogether in the new heaven and earth. Our hope in God is real even when bad things happen. How we process pain and suffering affects our worldview and our faith in God, which in turn determines our *moral* direction and *how* we live our lives.

CHAPTER 7

IS MORALITY RELATIVE?

Morality is always dreadfully complicated to a man who has lost all his principles. — G. K. Chesterton

When I was a boy in the early to mid-1970s, a friend's uncle was a member of the prestigious Playboy Bunny Club in New York City. I didn't really know what that meant, but I knew the family well. My friend's uncle seemed to love his wife, and the family seemed have strong moral values.

Years later, when I found out what the Playboy Club represented, I wondered why some perceived the Playboy enterprise to be something prestigious and positive. To be fair to my friend's uncle, in the '70s the Playboy Club was fairly modest. It functioned more like a social club than the sex-infested club it has become. The Playboy bunnies were simply young women who worked as waitstaff in the clubs.

From 1960 to 1986, there were forty Playboy nightclubs in the USA. During that time, the concept of a Playboy bunny transformed from waitstaff in clubs into Hugh Hefner's girlfriends who lived with him in the Playboy mansion. One of Hefner's ex-girlfriends, Holly Madison, wrote a tell-all book, *Down the Rabbit Hole: Curious Adventures and Cautionary Tales of a Former Playboy Bunny.* In an interview with *Business Insider*, she said, "Make no mistake, though—models who appear in *Playboy* magazine itself are 'playmates' not 'bunnies.'"[7]

In reaction to declining Playboy Club membership, the club changed the policy regarding attire: Playboy bunnies in the club could wear shorts once again (as opposed to being fully nude) because having fully nude women around 24/7 had lost its sense of mystique, which the Playboy Club equated with lower membership levels.

What effect did the advent of *Playboy* magazine have on American culture and the moral standards for cultures around the world? It started an immoral revolution against God and his moral, biblical standards by culturally redefining morality as relative.

HEFNER AND MORAL RELATIVISM

Although Playboy founder Hugh Hefner died on Wednesday, September 27, 2017, at the age of ninety-one, his life's work of morally relative mainstreaming porn lives on. It will continue to hurt men, women, and marriages for years to come. Furthermore, the *Playboy* magazine enterprise helped usher in an era of porn addiction, which has decreased happiness within countless marriages and strained relationships by turning erotic sexual behavior into a mainstream product that has contributed to the moral remaking of America and the world.

In his book, *Cheap Sex: The Transformation of Men, Marriage, and Monogamy*, University of Texas at Austin sociology professor Mark Regnerus notes that almost 40 percent of heterosexual men admit to viewing porn in the past six days. Regnerus also notes that viewing porn can have consequences for real-life behavior. For example, Regnerus spoke to a twenty-four-year-old named Jonathan from Austin, Texas. Jonathan said that using porn during relationships was an unfulfilling cycle, leaving him stressed and dissatisfied sexually with the person he was with.[2]

Porn's effects are not limited to males, though. Regnerus also spoke with women. Twenty-seven-year-old Alyssa from Milwaukee told him that she can see in herself the effect of watching porn. She said she feels a little bit sexier when she is having sex like a porn star but that porn sex is not . . . romantic. It is not seductive or slow; it is more thrusting and grunting than touching and sighing. She noted that the gentle loving aspect of making love is not hot in her estimation.[3]

How did we go from watching married couples on TV sitting in bed with sheets between them to having non-personal sex for pleasure and porn? This did not happen overnight or by accident. Hefner led America and the world on the road to moral relativism by planting the seeds of moral relativism in the minds of millions of men and women.

Moral relativism is the philosophical theory that all morality is relative. Moral relativism rejects the existence of absolute truth, ultimately rejecting any sense of an ultimate moral law. This leads to the rejection of God as the ultimate moral lawmaker and the conclusion that nothing can be determined morally right or wrong with absolute certainty. As a result, a particular behavior can be deemed right for you but not for me. Moral relativism holds to the belief that moral truth is not absolute or consistent for all people; rather, it can be defined differently by different cultures, subcultures, and religions according to experience, taste, and personal feelings.

In contrast, moral *absolutism* is an objective (not subjective) moral prescription. Moral absolutes are duty centered for all people; thus they are eternal as opposed to temporal obligations. Furthermore, moral absolutes are universal as a duty for all places and cultures. For example, it is absolutely wrong in every culture to commit murder.[4] This lies in stark contrast to moral relativism, which holds that a particular human behavior can be deemed right for one person but not for another. This leads us to ask the question, "How does one's thinking become relative to begin with?"

THE FROG IN THE KETTLE

Moral relativism does not typically occur in an immediate fashion. It is gradual, more like the boiling of a frog. The frog gets into or is put into the water. As the temperature increases, the frog cooks slowly—to the point that it does not even realize it is being boiled. It never sees the boil coming, and, eventually, it becomes a boiled frog.

Moral relativism also starts subtly. You are not asked to deny your morals flat out; you are encouraged to be flexible, give in just a bit on your absolute moral beliefs and positions. This flexibility is often presented in the name of compromise and tolerance. Can you feel the water warming? A little bit here and a little bit there, the water slowly boils your moral absolute worldview into one that insists morality is relative, and that it is intolerant to think otherwise!

When Hefner published his first issue of *Playboy* magazine in 1953, the moral climate in America was quite conservative: all fifty states could legally ban contraceptives and the word *pregnant* was not even allowed to air on the popular television program, *I Love Lucy*. *Playboy*'s first edition included nude pictures (taken years earlier) of Marilyn Monroe. In effort to soften Hefner's promotion of pornography within mainstream America, the Marilyn Monroe pictures were published with an editorial promise of "humor, sophistication, and spice." After all, if Hefner had called it what it was—pornography—few American men in 1953 would have looked at the magazine, much less subscribed to it. Within a year, circulation neared 200,000 and, within five years, grew to over one million. By the 1970s, *Playboy* magazine had more than seven million readers and inspired the inception of hard pornography magazines such as *Penthouse* and *Hustler*.

In 2017, sixty-four years after Hefner published his first *Playboy* issue, 38 percent of heterosexual men and nearly 7 percent of heterosexual women admit to viewing porn in the past six days.[5] How did this happen?

CULTURAL SUBJECTIVISM

Cultural subjectivism, or cultural relativism (used interchangeably), holds the position that individual human beliefs and activities are dictated by a person's culture. When culture, which is always changing, says that something is right or wrong for that particular culture, what is right and wrong becomes absolutely defined by that culture. A good example is the terrorist attacks on September 11, 2001. On that day, more than 3,000 innocent lives were lost at the hands of citizens from another culture because they held that their religious beliefs were right and superior to those held by citizens of the United States. Flying hijacked planes into two skyscrapers filled with unsuspecting people on a sunny September day is defined as acceptable to many radical Muslims because it fits their religious worldview. I have yet to hear anyone call a single one of those hijackers moral or cultural relativists. Most Americans believe the hijackers were absolutely wrong, even though the hijackers believed they were absolutely right.

One of the most dangerous post-9/11 threats to Western society is people who profess to be Christians but accept cultural relativism as true. Cultural relativism, which accepts the beliefs of the Muslim culture as true, strengthens the position of the 9/11 hijackers and weakens the Judeo-Christian position regarding what is right. In addition, it squelches the debate as to which religion is true.

Sharia Law (Islamic religious law) is a term used to designate a proper mode and norm of life in Islam as the proper way to live morally and in general.[6] The tolerance for Sharia Law in the United States is of concern to many for good reason. Islam, including many if not most Muslims, holds the belief that Sharia Law supersedes any other law, whether international or country specific, including the US Constitution. Despite this fact, some people in the United States and around the world still support the idea of cultural relativism, due in part to their lack of understanding about God, history, and reality. Many of these same people have no idea what they are condoning when they either fail to disagree with cultural relativism or proactively support it. By failing to adhere to moral absolutism, they open up a can of moral confusion.

Moral relativism takes the position that truth and morality cannot be absolute and therefore cannot be known with any certainty. Cultural subjectivism (relativism) assumes that truth and morality are relative and subjected to definition according to each person culture. In reality, culture does not create new frameworks of moral possibility; rather, it discovers, elaborates, and makes choices among possibilities already established within a given framework.

The ultimate moral framework was set in place in eternity by the God of truth, as found in biblical Scripture.

The most devastating effect of the acceptance of moral relativism as normative is in the lives of today's youth. For example, in a *Teen People* magazine interview, actor Brad Pitt gave the following response when answering a question about what defines the teenage years: "It's taking everything you've learned from your parents and school and finding out what works for you and what you have to offer. The important question is, 'What feels right for you?'"[7]

Allen Bloom (1930–1992) was a professor of classic literature at Cornell University, the University of Toronto, and Yale University. In *The Closing of the American Mind*, he wrote, "There is one thing a professor can be absolutely sure of: Almost every student entering the university believes, or says he believes, that truth is relative."[8] My response to that is, "Why believe anything your professor tells you if none of it is absolutely true?"

MORAL RELATIVISM'S BIG PROBLEM

The problem with moral relativism's claim regarding moral absolutism is that it is self-defeating. It claims that moral absolutism and objective morality do not exist and that all morality is relative, while at the same time it claims that its own view—morality is relative—is itself right and not relative. Put another way, moral relativists make the claim that objective morality does not exist and cannot be known, but they operate under the presumption that their own claims do exist and can be known.

Suppose you go to the bank to withdraw a million dollars, but you do not have a million dollars in your account. When the bank teller asserts that your balance is nowhere near that amount, can you legally receive a million dollars? Of course not. The relativist might think that the balance in his account is true for him but not for the bank teller; however, his view does not correspond to reality.

Many folks have embraced the self-defeating belief that if something is right for you it must be accepted by all of society as right, even if it is not right for them. The problem with this view is that moral absolutes are not created, changed, or defined by any single person, governmental body, or even mankind in general. Moral absolutes correspond to an ultimate standard in relation to the almighty God of the universe.

DENYINGMORAL ABSOLUTES CREATES CONFUSION

While nonbelievers, and even some within the church, seem to generally know that something—a rule, law, or philosophy—is wrong, many cannot put their finger on why it is wrong or what makes it wrong. Yet they can concede that our culture, country, and the world at large have a major moral sickness and that we seem to be spinning out of control without a moral compass. This has left many people desperately searching for solutions that will lead them back onto the right track and in the right direction. But moral relativism is the wrong road going in the wrong direction.

Because moral relativism cannot beat its opponent, moral absolutism, it seeks to confuse all sense of objectivity by labeling it as something changeable or unknowable. This has now affected all areas of our lives. Although we often cannot pinpoint or define the cause of the moral sickness that plagues our society, we can usually identify the outward symptoms. For example, those symptoms materialize through increasing violent crime, neighbors who do not look out for one another, and husbands and wives having affairs. While the moral sickness brought on by relativism through Adam and Eve in the Garden of Eden simmered over the centuries, it was vastly accelerated by the blatant rebellion against God in the 1950s and 1960s.

THE GREAT MORAL REBELLION

What started with Hugh Hefner's *Playboy* magazine in 1953 metastasized into a sexual revolution in 1969 at Woodstock, New York. This music festival was a rebellion against moral authority, whether that authority was God, parents, or government. The sexual revolution exerted a concerted effort to obtain liberation from any and all moral constraints. This eventually morphed into mainstream culture's explicit denial that moral absolutes exist. As a result of this moral rebellion, secular culture and many people within the church became infected with the false belief that morality is not absolute.

This rebellion ushered in a relative view about our sexual conduct, and it influenced many people's understanding of God's blueprint as the best and right model for the institution of marriage. Consequently, both the necessity and exclusivity of marital bonds were challenged. As the view of moral relativism expanded, traditional marriage, which had been defined since the beginning of time as a union between one man and one woman, was rejected as an institution ordained by God.

Other major societal institutions, ranging from government to business ethics, followed suit in subscribing to moral relativism. To see the fruits of this free fall, one needs only to read today's news headlines regarding every aspect of life, ranging from God to the state of marriage to government to Wall Street.

MORAL RELATIVITY IS A SIN PROBLEM

But moral relativism is not a Wall Street, governmental, or even a marital problem; it's a sin problem. People work for businesses. They also elect their government leaders, and because those government members are themselves sinners, they leave God out. When God is eliminated as the moral standard, all areas of life, leadership, and culture become infected by the immoral view that morality is defined by a changing, subjective standard. America's rejection of the God revealed in biblical Scriptures has seriously damaged the pillars of American culture. And the last pillar to be affected is the foundation of all American culture and institutions—the church.

THE FINAL STOP

Many people ask how the church in America has become such a weakened, nominally relevant body in a country founded on Judeo-Christian principles. The answer is that the church in recent decades has in great part been unwilling to take a stand for objective moral absolutes; consequently, it has failed to be salt and light in a deteriorating world. To reject God's moral principles is to reject America's core foundational beliefs, institutions, mores, and culture. As moral relativism has come full circle, this philosophy has influenced the church's growing rejection of the Bible as the authoritative Word of God, biblical morality as the sole objective standard, and Scripture as infallible. Many churches now view Scripture as fallible, adhering to the belief that the Bible is more folklore than the true Word of God.

As a result of the church's failure to be salt and light in the world, most every American institution ranging from traditional marriage to public education to the college university system to Hollywood has descended in an increasingly immoral direction.

THE CONSEQUENCES OF AN IRRELEVANT CHURCH

When Christians retreated from mainstream culture, many Christian leaders stopped preaching biblical absolutes as they relate to government policy and politics from the pulpit. And, as a result of a series of Supreme Court decisions beginning in the late 1940s and continuing into the 1980s, America's institutions and its culture have broken down. When Christians fail to be salt and light in any culture, that culture begins to be ruled by a limited group of people in the form of a secular government, as opposed to being led by a government of the people, by the people, and for the people. Any country or culture that chooses to change its national view from one nation under God to one nation without God eventually suppresses its freedom.

A CALL TO ACTION

History has shown over and over that when a society turns its back on God, God in turn passes judgment on that society. God's judgment often comes by way of him withdrawing his hand of blessing and protection on the nation that rejects him. America seems to be heading down the same road that ancient Rome traveled, even though we are a different country, a different people, and a different time. Is it too late for America? I do not believe so. But if the church does not wake up and take a stand, America will crumble just as the Roman Empire did.

How do we turn the ship around and learn to live according to moral absolutes in a relative age? That is the premise of this chapter. The answer lies with us as the unified, courageous body of Christ acting as salt and light in a dying world. We must be willing to diligently develop within ourselves, our children, and our community a commitment to the ultimate moral standard on which our nation was founded. We must raise up a new generation of believers who can influence those around them and who can address and dismantle the false, morally relative thought patterns of this age. We must equip Christians with a strong apologetics system and education so they can respond to moral relativism. Christians must now be equipped with the ability to give not only a biblical reason but also intellectual, theological, and logical reasons for the hope that lies within them (1 Peter 3:15).

THE TIME IS NOW

The time has come for all who subscribe to the Judeo-Christian moral code to stand up and stand strong for the moral principles on which America was founded. It would be wise for all of us individually and as a nation to understand, accept, and take responsibility for the moral slippery slope that we have slid down over the past sixty-plus years. From there, we need to be willing to take a stand for moral absolute principles.

The issue of moral absolutes and moral relativism is really the age-old struggle between darkness and light, good and evil. The real problem is not so much the darkness that now dominates our world but the absence of light in it. When light disappears, darkness is there, uninvited. The path of light toward God is the narrow path taken by few; the path of darkness is the wide path taken by many. It may take more courage to be light in today's age than in recent decades, but my hope is that every person will be courageous and open-minded enough to address the truth about moral relativism and to discover God's light in this world's darkness. For every human being on the face of the planet must choose between the path of light and the path of darkness.

HEFNER'S LEGACY

Hugh Hefner confessed in an interview with *Vanity Fair* in 2010 that he grew up in a home without "a lot of love or emotion." He said that the key to his life [was] the need to feel loved. When Hefner was asked in the interview who had broken his heart, he said it was the first girl he married. He also confessed that he was a very naïve person and that before he married his first wife, she confessed to him that she had an affair when he was in the army. He called her confession the most devastating experience of his life and said it doomed the marriage from the start. He also confessed that it gave him the permission to live the Playboy life he built for himself.[9]

As a result, even if Hefner was sincerely motivated in his work in developing the Playboy enterprise by his need to feel loved, he created a new world that championed lust over love. His legacy through the Playboy enterprise is men fantasizing about other women while they are with the women they actually love. It is also women preferring porn sex to romantic sex. The seeds of Hefner's first edition of *Playboy* magazine in 1953 have now grown into a culture struggling with sexually addictive behavior. What started as a "comical editorial" with a tad of spice in 1953 turned into an American staple for pornography, transforming American culture morally, leading to the sexual revolution in Woodstock in 1969. Soon after, no-fault divorce became acceptable and the law of the land, leading to a disregard for the institution of monogamous marriage as something archaic and outdated.

WHAT IF THE CHURCH WERE BETTER EQUIPPED?

There are both temporal and eternal consequences for holding to a morally relative view that defies God as the eternal ultimate Lawgiver as outlined in biblical Scriptures. I am thankful for your courage to examine moral relativism and to embark on the journey of how we can respond to the relativist's claim that moral absolutes do not exist. If you will approach what you have read in this chapter with an honest, open mind and seek to truly understand the issue of moral relativism, you will find that there are answers to the murky moral issues of life. It is my hope that you have been enlightened, encouraged, and equipped to respond to the claim that morality is relative, and that you will also help others discover moral absolutes in this relative age.

In an interview with Hollie McKay with Fox News in 2009 (eight years prior to his death), Hugh Hefner said that of all the Tinseltowners and tycoons who have entered the Playboy Mansion grounds and graced the pages of *Playboy* magazine, there is still one superstar he longs to meet:

"[I'd] like to find out what [Jesus Christ] was all about," he added. "Separate the reality from mythology. Find out the roots of what has become a major religion of my time. I was raised in a good Methodist home and I had questions about organized religion, and I would love to have the answers."[10]

Just think how different Hefner's life and his effect on American culture would have been if his parents had been equipped. Just think how different his life would have been if his school teacher, or anybody in his life, had been equipped to inoculate him for the morally relative hits that would come his way or had guided him from moral relativism back to moral absolutism later in life. If the church had been better equipped back then, the world today would be a more God-centered, morally absolute place.

[For more information on moral relativism, read *Right for You, But Not for Me: A Response to Moral Relativism* by Steven Garofalo. Available on Amazon.]

CHAPTER 8

HOW DO I KNOW THAT I AM GOING TO HEAVEN?

Your salvation depends on what [Christ] has done for you, not on what you do for him. It isn't your hold on God that saves you; it's his hold on you.[1] — Billy Graham

I recently added a rug to my home office, placing a beautiful black-and-beige rug on top of my off-white, stained carpet. A week later, I was shocked by how much dirt had accumulated on my new rug. I vacuumed the rug and my office promptly. Interestingly enough, the same thing happened the next week. We had purchased a fairly neutral rug for my office in an attempt to hide the dirt in the rug. The rug, however, was still dirty; it just did not look as dirty.

I thought about the wisdom of buying a neutral rug, or anything neutral for that matter, and concluded that for some things neutral is wise, but for other things it is unwise. For example, I buy neutral-colored automobiles. That is wise because the exterior of the car has no real impact on the sanitation of my living quarters. In other words, the car might be dirtier than it looks, but it does not affect my health or quality of life. Having a dirty carpet, on the other hand, is a different story. I sit on my carpet. I pray on my carpet. Sometimes I lie on my carpet. For many years, I have been lying on a very dirty carpet.

We face a similar problem in our walk with God. All of us probably have more dirt in our lives than we can see and more than we care to admit to and look at. How does the dirt (sin) of life become apparent in our lives? The Bible. The Bible tells us that we are all sinners in need of an ultimate, eternal cleansing and that only Jesus Christ, the Son of God, is able to offer us that through his atonement for our sins on the cross (1John 2:2). This leads us to ask an important question, "How do I know that I am clean enough before God to get into heaven?"

CAN I REALLY KNOW THAT I AM GOING TO HEAVEN?

Yes, absolutely. We can be sure about where we will spend eternity when we pass from this earth and our spirit leaves our body. We can know with certainty that when we die, we will go to heaven. How can we be sure? This is a question many people have struggled with, especially folks who are seeking God or who are new believers in Jesus Christ.

The Bible outlines how to have peace with God—it comes only through Jesus Christ. Most people have an idea of what they believe it will take to be accepted by God. After all, who likes the idea of exiting this life without being on good terms with God? Thankfully, it is possible to be certain that you have made peace with God, but the way must be chosen during this life. Here are the steps drawn from God's book, the Bible, laid out by the Billy Graham Evangelistic Association.

STEPS TO PEACE WITH GOD:

The Bible teaches that the assurance of salvation our unshakable pillars:

STEP 1.
UNDERSTAND GOD'S PURPOSES—PEACE AND ETERNAL LIFE.

God loves you and wants you to experience peace and eternal, fulfilling life.

The Bible says ...

We have peace with God through our Lord Jesus Christ. (Romans 5:1)

For God so loved the world, that he gave his only Son, that whoever believes in him should not perish but have eternal life. (John 3:16)

Jesus said, "*I came that they may have life and have it abundantly.*" (John 10:10)

Why don't most people have this peace and the fulfilling (abundant) life that God intended for us to have?

STEP 2.
ADMIT THE PROBLEM—OUR SIN AND SEPARATION.

God did not create us like robots to automatically love and mechanically obey him. God gave us a will and the freedom to choose. The first man and woman chose to disobey God and go their own willful way. And we still make that choice today. This results in separation from God.

The Bible says ...

For all have sinned and fall short of the glory of God. (Romans 3:23)

For the wages of sin is death. Romans 6:23

People have tried many ways to bridge this gap between themselves and God.

The Bible says ...

There is a way that seems right to a man, but its end is the way to death. (Proverbs 14:12)

Your iniquities have made a separation between you and your God ... (Isaiah 59:2)

No bridge reaches God ... except one.

STEP 3.
DISCOVER GOD'S BRIDGE—THE CROSS.

Jesus Christ died on the cross and rose from the grave. Though he was God's sinless Son, he became a human, took our place, and paid the penalty for our sin, bridging the gap between God and us.

The Bible says ...

For there is one God, and there is one mediator between God and men, the man Christ Jesus. (1 Timothy 2:5)

Christ ... suffered once for sins, the righteous for the unrighteous, that he might bring us to God. (1 Peter 3:18)

God shows his love for us in that while we were still sinners, Christ died for us ... the free gift of God is eternal life in Christ Jesus our Lord. (Romans 5:8; Romans 3:23)

Christ died for our sins ... he was buried ... he was raised on the third day. (1 Corinthians 15:3–4)

God has provided the only way to forgiveness of sin and eternal life. But each person must make a choice.

STEP 4. EMBRACE THE TRUTH—RECEIVE CHRIST.

We must trust Jesus Christ as our Savior and receive him by personal choice.

Jesus says ...

"Behold, I stand at the door and knock. If anyone hears my voice and opens the door, I will come in and eat with him, and he with me." (Revelation 3:20)

"I am the way, and the truth, and the life. No one comes to the Father except through me." (John 14:6)

The Bible says ...

To all who did receive him, who believed in his name, he gave the right to become children of God. (John 1:12)

Whoever believes in the Son has eternal life. (John 3:36)

WHAT IS YOUR DECISION?

Will you receive Jesus Christ right now and trust in him alone for forgiveness and eternal life? The Bible says that's the only way to find peace with God!

- Admit your need—that you are a sinner in need of God's forgiveness.
- Be willing to turn from trusting in anything else for eternal life and trust only in Christ.
- Believe that Jesus Christ died for you on the cross, came back to life from the grave, and is your only way to heaven.
- Accept Jesus' offer to forgive your sins and come into your life as your Savior.

You may want to tell him in words like these:

Dear Jesus, thank you for making it possible for me to find peace with God! I believe that when you died you were paying the penalty for my sins. I now receive you into my life as my Savior, so I can have forgiveness and never-ending life from God! Thank you for the gift of eternal life![2]

CHAPTER 9

HOW DO I USE APOLOGETICS TO DEFEND THE CHRISTIAN FAITH?

It is not hard to find the truth. What is hard is not to run away from it once you have found it. —Etienne Gilson

Apologetics is a branch of theology devoted to the defense of the divine origin and authority of Christianity.[1] In *5-Minute Apologetics for Today*, author and speaker Dr. Ron Rhodes writes, "Our country has become a virtual cafeteria of different religions, cults, and non-Christian worldviews that are all vying for supremacy on America's religious landscape. ... We need Christian wisdom and biblical discernment as never before."[2] In other words, America has become part of the global economy, which, in turn, has opened the door for America to be subjected to global religiosity. As a result, the necessity for apologetics as a tool for evangelism and for giving a defense of the Christian faith is more important today than ever.

Apologetics in *evangelism* helps unbelievers form more truthful beliefs about God, the Bible, and Christianity. Apologetics in *defense* of the Bible helps defuse attacks on Christianity, establishing its credibility through scientific, scriptural, logical, archeological, and other types of evidence. Apologetics addresses head on subjective questions such as how one knows anything (including the existence of God), why God allows evil, and the unique salvific message of Jesus Christ as the exclusive truth and means of salvation. My mentor, author and speaker Dr. Norman Geisler, put it this way:

> *The heart of this apologetic approach is that the Christian is interested in defending the truths that Christ is the Son of God and the Bible is the Word of God. However, prior to establishing these two pillars on which the uniqueness of Christianity is built, one must establish the existence of God. It makes no sense to speak about an act of God (i.e., a miracle) confirming that Christ is the Son of God and that the Bible is the Word of God unless, of course, there is a God who can have a Son and who can speak a Word.*[3]

Whether evangelizing, reasoning from the Scriptures, or defending the Christian faith, you will inevitably encounter intellectual objections that must be answered. Knowing how to effectively respond to those objections is essential. In this chapter, we will focus on how to handle the interpersonal interaction of evangelism and defending the Christian faith. The prior eight chapters equipped you to answer some of the most common objections to Christianity and attacks against it. This chapter provides you with some strategic, tactical ways to apply what you have learned thus far. The more we know about the truth and the facts, the *less we will argue from emotion.* The less we know about the truth and the facts, the *more we will argue from emotion.* I trust these strategies will help you respond with truth rather than emotion.

It can be difficult to rationalize with someone who is making irrational arguments or giving you false truth claims. As my first seminary professor told me when I pressed him on that issue, "Steve, you cannot rationalize with an irrational person or a person acting irrationally." While we cannot win every argument or soul for Christ, we can always give a well-informed answer that makes people think about the truth.

RATIONALIZING WITH SOMEONE ACTING IRRATIONAL

One day while I was working out at the YMCA, a regular attendee at the gym approached me (unsolicited) and challenged me regarding my position on Christianity as the only way to heaven. I reasoned with him from the Scriptures using apologetics for quite some time before I realized that his ideology was stronger than his rationality, which rendered truth irrelevant in our discussion about God and eternity. He challenged me regarding the existence of God, absolute truth, and the exclusivity of salvation found in Jesus Christ. He asked me how I knew anything was true or right (two different things). After some time, I finally asked him, "Do you exist?"

He thought about that for a moment before giving his answer. He could give three possible responses: "yes," "no," or "I don't know." If he said yes or no, he would admit to believing in truth as absolute and knowable; therefore, he gave the typical ideological and irrational response, which is "I don't know." By using this relative answer, he did not have to admit that some knowledge was absolute. In other words, if he said yes or no, he would be acknowledging that absolute truth exists and can be known. If truth is absolute and can be known, then we can know the absolute truth that God exists. Such a commitment would open the door to acknowledging Jesus Christ as Lord and Savior and the exclusive way to the Father and heaven. When he said, "I don't know if I exist," he erred in that he presumed his own proclamations and denials were absolute truth, which is a self-defeating philosophical stance.

Next, he assumed a relative position regarding right or wrong, which relates to morality and ethics. He proclaimed that we cannot know if anything is right or wrong. After all, if truth cannot be known, then the existence of God cannot be known. If we cannot know if God exists, then we are not accountable to the words of Jesus and would not have to adhere to the moral principles as laid out in the Bible. That was his challenge to me.

Before moving on with the conversation, I asked him, "If truth is relative and nothing can be known absolutely, how can anything you say be absolutely truthful or even knowable?" He didn't have an answer. He was not a mean guy, just a mixed-up, lost guy. My goal was not to win the argument but to show him the irrational nature of his ideology, which defied logic, truth, and reality. To deny God's existence was rebellious, but to deny his own existence was insanity!

Out of that experience, I came up with a three-stage strategic plan for using apologetics to defend the truth in pre-evangelism conversations.

USING APOLOGETICS IN EVANGELISM: A THREE-STAGE STRATEGIC PLAN

These three stages of strategic response are not something conjured up out of theory. Rather, they comprise a simple strategy that we use in our everyday lives when making a point or defending something that we believe to be true. The specific topics will vary with audience and time, but how those points are made, argued, and discussed, remain the same.

- Stage One. Ask God for the wisdom and the words. Scripture is clear that God will give you the words to say if you are prayed up and prepared.
- Stage Two. Use the *Road Runner Tactic,* a term coined by Dr. Norman Geisler and Frank Turek for turning an untruthful and illogical argument back on itself in an effort to expose it as self-defeating.
- Stage Three. Understand how the *Shell Game* is played, and take control of the game to expose the truth and respond to numerous hit-and-run assertions with rational conversation. What are hit-and-run assertions? When people argue from emotion, they tend

to use a continuous barrage of quick but false assertions based on false assumptions. Because the assertions are made in rapid succession, you have no chance to respond, so the invalidated assertions are left unanswered and unchallenged.

STEP ONE: ASK GOD FOR THE WISDOM AND THE WORDS

When you enter a discussion regarding God and Christianity, you will automatically enter an unseen spiritual battle. The apostle Paul wrote about this unseen spiritual battleground while he was imprisoned in Rome:

> *Finally, be strong in the Lord, and in the strength of his might. Put on the full armor of God, so that you may be able to stand firm against the schemes of the devil. For our struggle is not against flesh and blood, but against the rulers, against the powers, against the world forces of this darkness, against the spiritual forces of wickedness in the heavenly places. Therefore, take up the full armor of God, that you may be able to resist in the evil day, and having done everything, to stand firm."* (Ephesians 6:10–13, NASB)

When you begin to evangelize or defend the Christian faith, you will be elevated to a new, higher level of spiritual warfare; therefore, prepare to be in the center of that unseen spiritual battle. The first thing you want to do is to ask God for two specific things he has promised to provide: the words to use and the wisdom to respond. In his gospel, Luke writes that we are to be dependent on God for the words we need to stand strong when entering such a battle and giving a response:

> *But before all this they will lay their hands on you and persecute you, delivering you up to the synagogues and prisons, and you will be brought before kings and governors for my name's sake. This will be your opportunity to bear witness. Settle it therefore in your minds not to meditate beforehand how to answer, for I will give you a mouth and wisdom, which none of your adversaries will be able to withstand or contradict.* (Luke 21:12–15, ESV)

It is important to interpret and understand Luke 21 in its correct context. We have been called to be in the Word of God on a daily basis and to learn the Scriptures in preparation to be used by God. How will we be given the right words at the right time if we are not familiar with the Scriptures? God gives people who are consistently in the Scriptures the right words and wisdom. But how will he do this if we do not know the Word to begin with?

We must be more like a well-trained athlete or a disciplined soldier than an undisciplined, occasional, or weekend athlete or soldier. This was Paul's point to Timothy:

> *You then, my son, be strong in the grace that is in Christ Jesus. And the things you have heard me say in the presence of many witnesses entrust to reliable people who will also be qualified to teach others. Join with me in suffering, like a good soldier of Christ Jesus. No one serving as a soldier gets entangled in civilian affairs, but rather tries to please his commanding officer. Similarly, anyone who competes as an athlete does not receive the victor's crown except by competing according to the rules. The hardworking farmer should be the first to receive a share of the crops. Reflect on what I am saying, for the Lord will give you insight into all this.* (2 Timothy 2:1–7)

What sports team or military outfit would use an untrained, undisciplined, or unfit person? You do not need a seminary degree to be used of God. Neither do you need to be a pastor, preacher, or a priest. God uses ordinary, committed people like you and me to do his business. He uses the ordinary to do the extraordinary. If you, like a well-trained soldier or athlete, read God's Word and pray daily, he will use you. He will give you the words and extraordinary wisdom to answer the most intelligent of questions.

Paul speaks to this in 1 Corinthians: *For the word of the cross is folly to those who are perishing, but to us who are being saved it is the power of God. For it is written, "I will destroy the wisdom of the wise, and the discernment of the discerning I will thwart"* (1:18–19, ESV). If you are faithful with the Scriptures and obtain some Christian apologetics training, God will use you in more impactful ways. If you seek God in prayer and in his Word as a regular part of your spiritual diet, God will use you in ways that may amaze you.

Keep in mind that we are simply the *messengers*, not the message itself. When our message is rejected, we are not being rejected; it's the truth about God and his Word that someone is rejecting. Jesus said, "*Whoever listens to you listens to me; whoever rejects you rejects me; but whoever rejects me rejects him who sent me*" (Luke 10:16). Our job is to seek out where people are in their spiritual journey with God and to love those who may not know the truth. Remember, this is a battle for souls, and the real enemy, Satan, has blinded unbelievers. We should be able to gauge where a person is spiritually and then answer questions accordingly.

Now that we understand that God will give us words and wisdom our adversary cannot contradict, let's move on to the second stage, the Road Runner Tactic. Here we learn how to apply truth and logic to the conversation to expose false statements and shed light on our truth claims.

STAGE TWO: HOW TO TURN AN ARGUMENT ON ITS HEAD

The second stage of the responsive strategy of using apologetics in conversational evangelism is to turn a self-defeating, illogical argument on its head using the *Road Runner Tactic.* The Road Runner Tactic is named after the cartoon characters Road Runner and Wile E. Coyote. If you are unfamiliar with Road Runner and Wile E. Coyote, look them up on Google or YouTube. Their antics will amuse you. In the cartoons, Wile E. Coyote's only goal in life is to chase down Road Runner and make the speedy bird his next meal. The problem, though, is that Road Runner is simply too fast and too smart. He eludes the persistent coyote at every turn. Every time the coyote gains ground, Road Runner stops short at a cliff or some other impasse. As a result, Wile E. Coyote passes him and ends up suspended in mid-air just long enough to look into the camera and affirm that he is supported by ... nothing. He then plummets to the valley floor below.[4]

This is precisely what the Road Runner Tactic can do with false arguments when defending your faith. This tactic helps us show others that their arguments do not stand up under their own weight and convictions; it turns a false argument on its head by subjecting it to its own logical principles. This is an essential tactic to use, especially for college students.

Examples of using the Road Runner Tactic are as follows:

- "All truth is relative" (Is that a *relative* truth?)
- "There are no absolutes" (Are you *absolutely* sure?)
- "Only science gives us the truth" (Is that a *scientific* truth?)
- And everybody's favorite, "It's true for you but not for me" (Is that statement true just for you, or is it true for everyone?)

These false mantras are false for one simple reason: they are self-defeating.[5]

The above statements are guilty of what we might call the wise man's perspective in the Indian fable presented in chapter three. To conclude that all the blind men are partially correct requires the presence of a wise man who sees clearly. In the same way, a person who declares no one knows the truth is making a self-defeating assertion.

DID JESUS AND OTHER BIBLICAL CHARACTERS USE THE ROAD RUNNER TACTIC?

I assert that Jesus Christ often used the Road Runner Tactic, or self-defeating logic, to expose the truth with those who attempted to trap him in his own words. For example, Jesus often answered a question with another question. He used this common rabbinical practice to expose the hypocrisy and self-defeating position of the Pharisees and other religious leaders.

Consider the following example from the book of Matthew. Jesus is responding to the chief priests and elders who challenged him on the source of his authority:

And when he entered the temple, the chief priests and the elders of the peo-

ple came up to him as he was teaching, and said, "By what authority are you doing these things, and who gave you this authority?" Jesus answered them, "I also will ask you one question, and if you tell me the answer, then I also will tell you by what authority I do these things. The baptism of John, from where did it come? From heaven or from man?" And they discussed it among themselves, saying, "If we say, 'From heaven,' he will say to us, 'Why then did you not believe him?' But if we say, 'From man,' we are afraid of the crowd, for they all hold that John was a prophet." So they answered Jesus, "We do not know." And he said to them, "Neither will I tell you by what authority I do these things." (Matthew 21:23–27, ESV)

Jesus used logic and truth in defending the truth of the authority of God and his position as the Son of God. The Pharisees were as bamboozled as Wile E. Coyote. As Road Runner would say, "Beep! Beep!"

Jesus did not always recite Scripture or strictly use logic and truth when responding to questions or teaching about God or his own role as the Son of God. Jesus often used one or the other and sometimes combined them. We can learn much from the way Jesus responded to people, using a combination of Scripture, logic, teaching, and evangelistic preaching. God not only gives us the words but also the discernment, proper recall of Scripture, and wisdom to give a logical, true response that will expose the darkness with his light.

Like Jesus, you can use self-defeating logic (the Road Runner Tactic) to expose the truth with those who attempt to trap you in your own words by answering a question with another question. You can remove obstacles to the Christian faith and expose the self-defeating position of the many false arguments and hidden fallacies that you encounter daily in fulfilling the Great Commission. Our part is to be prepared to give a response for the hope that lies within us (1 Peter 3:15).

STAGE THREE: STOPPING THE SHELL GAME

But what happens when you encounter a person who rapidly makes all their points without letting you to get a word in? I call this the Shell Game Tactic. The original Shell Game involves a sleight-of-hand artist placing an object under one of three inverted cups or nutshells, then moving them around. The other person must spot which shell conceals the object. The shell game is also played, often unintentionally, when a person tries to make and win an argument with a bunch of empty arguments (shells).

Stage Three of the responsive strategy is to learn how the Shell Game is played in an effort to clarify confusing talking points. The strategy begins with Stages One and Two: asking God to provide the right words and wisdom, followed by using logic through the Road Runner Tactic. These two stages provide a framework that will allow you to implement Stage Three and respond to each relative statement.

When the person you are speaking with dominates the conversation—firing one assertion after another without giving you the opportunity to respond to any of their objections—you have to stop the Shell Game and redirect the conversation in a fair, truthful, and orderly fashion. To stop the Shell Game, you need to effectively answer false arguments before they become so numerous that they are perceived as the truth for no other reason than that they were not answered. This is an essential tactic in evangelism, discussion, and debate.

Stopping the continuous flow of untruthful and deceptive assertions will allow you the opportunity to respond. The goal is to address the person's objections one assertion at a time. Have you ever seen a television roundtable discussion or debate in which one person dominates the discussion with a slew of assertions so the others cannot get a word in edgewise? When the other person attempts to dominate the conversation, we must kindly blow the referee whistle and stop the conversation long enough to answer the objections thrown at us. The way to do this is to understand and master a few basic techniques.

STEP ONE: STOP THE RUNAWAY TRAIN AND ADDRESS THE ASSERTIONS

The first step in stopping the Shell Game is to kindly but assertively stop the runaway train of assertions so you can respond. Do this kindly, assertively, and naturally. By affirming your empathy through body language and voice inflection that you have heard the other person, you create the opportunity to be heard yourself. If you are unwilling to stop the Shell Game, you will probably lose the game by default because you will not be able to make your own points.

Even if you get to answer one objection at some point, the other person usually ends up leading the discussion through other assertions while you only make one or two points. Successfully defending your faith starts with your willingness to engage an unbeliever in an attempt to answer their questions. Like most things in life, practice makes perfect. As you engage with nonbelievers, you will become more prepared for tactics like the Shell Game. If you are unable to stop the Shell Game, the other person will assume there are no good answers to their questions about Christianity or their objections to it. By stopping their barrage of assertions, you open the door for the second step, which is to affirm the other person.

STEP TWO: UNDERSTAND, EMPATHIZE, AND AFFIRM

The second step in stopping the Shell Game is to let the other person know you care about what they say by affirming that you are genuinely listening. The idea is not to win the argument at the expense of further alienating an unbeliever from God. The point is to share God's love and move that person closer Jesus Christ. You may want to consciously nod your head to visually affirm you have heard the other person, acknowledging that they have made some excellent points. If nothing else, you can compliment them on their willingness to speculate about matters of God, faith, and the afterlife. Next, tell them you would like to address one of their points before moving on their other objections and talking points. Note that their concerns may orbit around a central theme such as why God allows evil, pain, and suffering. In that case, do not get bogged down in answering specific questions. Take a step back and try to address this larger issue by saying something like this: "It seems like you are really concerned as to why a loving God would allow the kind of pain and suffering we see in the world." This will sometimes unearth a deep emotional wound that is causing that person to resist God's love. By affirming that their opinion counts, you are treating them like an individual, and you are demonstrating that you care about them as a person. In most cases, you will earn their respect. Listening to them demonstrates that you authentically care about what they have to say as opposed to simply wanting to argue with them.

STEP THREE: RESPOND TO THE OBJECTIVES, OBSTACLES, AND ARGUMENTS

The third step in stopping the Shell Game is to give a response. In many cases, you will know more about the issues, the nature of truth, and the Scripture than those with whom you are speaking. Much of the progress made here will be related to correcting some of their misunderstandings about Christianity. When you are reasoning from the Scriptures or defending the truth, the other person will often attempt to play the Shell Game. Sometimes it will be a fast and furious game of non-stop objections hurled at you in aggressive fashion. But at other times, the Shell Game will manifest itself in a simple, innocent objection about who God is, the nature of truth, the accuracy of the Bible, or the person of Jesus Christ. The underlying truth is that people do not want to *come into the light for fear that their evil deeds will be exposed* (John 3:20). When unbelievers play the Shell Game, their minds are often blinded to the truth of God. You can pray that the Holy Spirit breaks through their darkness and opens their mind and heart to the truth. Your task is to demonstrate that Christianity is reasonable and that Jesus Christ is alive in your heart, mind, and life. You can do this with a display of intelligence, love, and compassion.

In many cases, once the Shell Game has been stopped long enough for the individual statements and false assertions (shells) to be addressed, the person playing the game will respond positively. Why? Using the principles of truth and logic appeals to people's natural inclination to want to know the truth. Folks often choose to *reject* the truth, but everyone wants to *know* the truth.

Most people will appreciate and respect the fact that you bring reason and truth into the conversation. After years of hearing the mantra of relativism preached repeatedly, some people have been conditioned to believe truth is relative. Therefore, they find statements of absolute truth pleasant and refreshing. Others will adamantly deny the truth. In those cases, you may be the first person to crack the façade of lies that encases their heart and mind. God may be using you to help someone think about the truth of God in Jesus Christ. Like evangelism, some are called to plant seeds while others are called to reap the crops (John 4:34–38). Defending the truth is no different.

WARNING: THE DANGER OF FAILING TO LEARN AND PLAY THE SHELL GAME

Failing to learn how to play the Shell Game will leave you ill equipped to defend the truth of God and biblical principles, which gives the father of lies, Satan, freedom to distort the truth about God. When you reason in truth with others, you will sometimes converse with people who argue from emotion and opinion as opposed to reasoning from knowledge, facts, and truth. In those cases, understand that the person may not have the evidence or a solid logical basis to back up their claims. As a result, they are cornered, with no other option than to base their assertions on opinion and emotion. They move on to other assertions, also based on opinion and emotion, to avoid logically and truthfully explaining their previous assertions. Emotions, experience, and opinions have nothing to do with determining the truth because truth corresponds to reality and "the way it is" despite how anybody feels about it. Some people will not like hearing that fact, but it is true for both you and me. Truth cuts through relativism like sunlight in a dark room. That is why it is important to stop the other person's Shell Game and affirm that you have heard their talking points and value their opinion.

Nothing is more arduous than having to explain your assertion when you do not possess a truthful answer to begin with. In most (not all) cases when people argue from emotion, they usually do so for no other reason than the fact that they have nothing else to argue from. As a result, people adhering to the position of relativism argue from the flawed, false arguments they have been fed by the multitude of relative, liberal-leaning media sources, trusting that what they have heard is the truth. This is what differentiates an educated opinion from an emotional opinion. Emotions and personal experience do not define what is true from what is not true. Our five senses can fail to tell us the truth; thus they cannot be relied on to define the truth. Emotions can support the truth, but they do not determine or define it.

IN CONCLUSION

Let's go back to my friend at the YMCA who denied absolute truth, the existence of God, and his own existence. If I had not used apologetics, the Bible and Christianity would have appeared without merit outside of their own claims. Toward the end of my conversation with that gentleman, I asked, "Is murder is right or wrong?"

He paused and then said, "It depends."

I clarified that I was speaking about first-degree, premeditated murder.

He again replied, "It depends."

"Depends on what?" I countered.

"The person's background, upbringing, socio-economic status, etc."

"So," I probed, "who determines if murder is right or wrong?"

"The US Congress makes those laws."

"Then where does Congress get its authority from and where does it get those laws from?"

He responded correctly, "England."

I wanted to show him that God is the ultimate authority as to what is right and wrong. I explained that all US laws are based on what is known as Common Law, which we brought with us from England.

While Common Law came from England, it literally is the Ten Commandments. The US Supreme Court has the Ten Commandments etched in stone on the top of the walls inside the courtroom and on many of the doors and walls within the US Supreme Court building.

In attempt to help him see the irrationality in his ideology, I then asked him how his young son and daughter were doing. He perked up and said, "They're doing great! Thank you for asking."

I then asked him a simple but crude question to illustrate the seriousness of his relative position. "Sir, what if a convicted felon came into your home and raped and murdered your family. Is that right or wrong?"

"That's disgusting!" he said.

"I totally agree."

He had no real response because he was checkmated by the laws of logic and his own words. I then told him that under his ideological beliefs, if somebody walked into the room at that moment and murdered him, there would be nothing wrong or illegal in that person's actions for two reasons. First, if the murderer believed it was right to kill him, he could not say it was wrong since right and wrong are relative. Second, I told him that no murder charges could be filed legally because he is not sure he even exists.

He lowered his head because he saw the irrational, illogical, untrue nature of his position on absolute truth and moral absolutes.

We live in a postmodern culture, which is led by social media and mainstream media talking points as opposed to truth and reason. If we are to be effective in our presentation of the good news of Jesus Christ, we must intertwine apologetics and evangelism rather than treat them as separate disciplines. Anyone who has tried to share their faith in recent years will most likely agree that affirming Christianity opens one up to both hostility and a host of questions. The biblical view of reality is increasingly disregarded by society. It is popular for people to reject wholesale any version of organized religion, even if they are interested in spiritual matters. By combining apologetics with our evangelistic efforts we can, by God's grace, move these individuals from their vague interest in spirituality to a more specific interest in the claims of Jesus and Christianity. That is the subject of the next chapter, which addresses using apologetics in conversational evangelism.

CHAPTER 10

HOW CAN I USE APOLOGETICS IN CONVERSATIONAL PRE-EVANGELISM?

CARRYING OUT THE GREAT COMMISSION IN A POSTMODERN AGE

Evangelism is not a calling reserved exclusively for the clergy. I believe one of the greatest priorities of the church today is to mobilize the laity to do the work of evangelism.[1] —Billy Graham

Shortly after world-renowned evangelist Billy Graham passed away on February 21, 2018, Graham's personal pastor, the Rev. Dr. Don Wilton, spoke of the importance of all Christians being evangelists for God's kingdom in an article written by CBN titled "Three Things Christians Should Pray for Ahead of Billy Graham's Funeral." Dr. Wilton said, "We need all to understand that we're all called to be evangelists. We are all witnesses. ... We are all people that are told to go out into all the world and share the love of Christ. What greater treasure could there be?"[2]

Evangelism is the responsibility for all believers, not solely the job of the church or any professional ministry. Using apologetics in conversational evangelism is essential for sharing our faith in the modern age, starting with pre-evangelism. Pre-evangelism precedes conversational evangelism because, in most cases, when we share our faith, we'll more likely than not have to address difficult theological and philosophical questions to remove obstacles people have erected against the Christian faith.

Apologetics in and of itself is not the gospel, but it can be used as an effective tool for eliminating whatever obstacles may prohibit a person from considering the Christian faith, which may lead to their salvation. A hunter uses camouflage to disguise himself in the wild much as people hide behind erroneous philosophies, but apologetics can pull back that camouflage, revealing the truth about false world religions and false ideas about the Bible, Jesus Christ, and Christianity. Apologetics enables us to help others uncover the true nature of the gospel, which is increasingly being obscured by immoral governmental policies, false religions, and false worldviews. The starting point for overcoming these obstacles is to be equipped with apologetics and pre-evangelism tools.

Using apologetics with pre-evangelism and conversational evangelism is a powerful combination. By uniting them, you will be far more effective in removing intellectual and emotion obstacles that impede others from trusting in Jesus Christ; prayer, however, is what unleashes the Holy Spirit to convict the heart of the person with whom you are speaking. We cannot change someone's heart, but the Holy Spirit can. What we can do is use apologetics in pre-evangelism and conversational evangelism to lead others to eternal salvation in Jesus Christ.[3]

As Reverend Wilton said, evangelism is the job of *all* Christians, not just the trained pastor, priest, or professional evangelist. It is our job—mine and yours. It is our responsibility to be in the Word of God daily and to be equipped with apologetics so we may better execute the Great Commission (Matthew 28:16–20) in the twenty-first century.

SHARING YOUR FAITH IN THE REAL WORLD

Years ago, I worked for a computer software company in Washington, DC. While I was employed there, the top computer scientist challenged me vehemently regarding my faith in Jesus Christ. As it turned out, he was an atheist. He aggressively came after me with great tenacity and intensity. In turn, I answered him kindly but firmly with facts and Scripture. With great passion and a bit of anger, this top scientist demanded that I state the exact year that dinosaurs roamed the earth. Not a time frame, but an exact year. This was an obvious attempt to make me, a Christian, look foolish and Christianity look false. I repeatedly told him that I would not commit to an exact year, but he kept pressing me for a specific date. After some time, another computer scientist who worked with us stepped in and said rather directly to the first computer scientist, "Leave him alone. He already told you that he doesn't want to give you an exact date."

What was interesting is that the second computer scientist, who stood up for me, had an interesting worldview that was very different from mine and the other computer scientist. The man who supported my stance was an American-born US citizen whose dad was an American contractor for the US government. This computer scientist lived in Turkey the first ten years of his life. His parents told him that they didn't want to teach him anything about truth or God because they wanted him to determine for himself if God existed and the truth about religion.

When I asked him what he believed about God and the origins of life, he told me that he believed aliens dropped us (the human race) off on Planet Earth and that was how we got here. I did not laugh at him or give him a shocked look. I said, "Cool! I want to hear about your thoughts on aliens, and I'd like to share what I know about Jesus and the Bible." We had a very nice conversation that continued after everyone left the conference room where we all ate lunch. But before the room emptied, I realized I had gained the attention of the entire company—about thirty people.

Looking back, I was sharing my faith through conversational evangelism. From the receptionist from Barbados to the computer scientists to the salespeople and administrators, the gospel was being proclaimed through everyday relationships and conversational evangelism. Through that experience, I discovered six guideposts for using apologetics in pre-evangelism and conversational evangelism.

SIX GUIDEPOSTS FOR USING APOLOGETICS IN EVANGELISM

A guidepost is a sign placed on the roadside or at an intersection, which offers guidance for travelers. Similarly, we can use biblical guideposts to help us share the good news of Jesus Christ with others. Although he Bible contains many guideposts for using apologetics in evangelism, the six I have selected will help you to be more effective when you share your faith in pre-evangelism and conversational evangelism.

The first guidepost is *to make our starting point the greatest commandment.* Jesus gave us what he designated as the greatest commandment: *"Love the Lord your God with all your heart and with all your soul and with all your mind"* (see Matthew 22:36–40). It's important for us to seek God first in all things—including our starting point for evangelism—with all our heart, mind, and soul. Luke's account adds our strength as well (Luke 10:27).

Scripture tells us that we must not ignore loving God with either heart or mind; rather, we must pursue and love God with *all* our heart, mind, soul, and strength. But sometimes we want to love others into God's kingdom with only our heart and not our mind; other times we want to reason with others with our mind, while ignoring the heart. But Jesus clearly said it is not either-or but both-and. This puts us in the correct frame of heart and mind. To ignore one or the other will limit our efforts in sharing our faith with others. Out of this first guidepost, the remaining five guideposts flow.

The second guidepost is *to be in prayer daily.* Start each day in prayer, then pray throughout the day, keeping short tabs with God. When we are sharing our faith with others, we should silently pray both for the right words to say and for the person with whom we are speaking. When we share our faith with non-Christians, we become a potential threat in that we are taking away from the Enemy's team to add to God's team. This means conflict between the kingdom of darkness and the kingdom of light. Without prayer, our efforts are limited. Prayer transfers our reliance on ourselves to a reliance on God for the right words and the outcome of our efforts. God will give us the right words to say while the Holy Spirit interacts with the heart of the person listening to us. Jesus said, *"for the Holy Spirit will teach you at that time what you should say"* (Luke 12:12). This is the focus of the third post.

The third guidepost is *to ask God to open the heart of the other person.* We have to depend on the Holy Spirit as the only Person who can change someone's heart. God tells us, *"I will give you a new heart and put a new spirit in you; I will remove from you your heart of stone and give you a heart of flesh"* (Ezekiel 36:26). We can be obedient and deliver the gospel message, but as humans we cannot change another person's heart. Accepting this truth frees us to do what the Lord has called us to do in evangelism using apologetics without the responsibility of the hearer immediately accepting our words.

The fourth guidepost is *to stay in the Word of God daily,* studying and learning the Scriptures. We cannot give what we do not have, and we will not keep what we do not use. The adage, "use it or lose it," applies to studying God's Word on a regular basis. Scripture tells us, *All Scripture is breathed out by God and profitable for teaching, for reproof, for correction, and for training in righteousness, that the man of God may be complete, equipped for every good work* (2 Timothy 3:16–17, ESV). The key word is *equipped.* Being in the Word of God will equip us to effectively share the Word of God with others. Apologetics can accent but not replace the Word of God as the primary tool for evangelism.

The fifth guidepost is *to be diligent and proactive in identifying with other people*. If the person you are sharing with likes NASCAR and you like NASCAR, make that a starting point for connecting with him or her. If you like cooking or gardening, make that your starting point. Most people are spiritual in the broad sense of believing in a Divine Presence, forces of good and evil, angelic beings, and supernatural events, which allows us as Christians to connect with them on a spiritual level. Sometimes, though, we must find something more specific, sometimes more secular, that we have in common with them to move the conversation in a spiritual direction. When sharing your faith with others, first establish some commonalities with them; build bridges to their heart and mind as a starting point.

The sixth and final guidepost is *to be a willing vessel* so the Lord can use you in his plan for the person with whom you are speaking as well as for yourself. We want to be in God's will, and that entails stepping out in faith and courage when sharing our faith. How else will others hear the good news of Jesus Christ if we as Christians are not willing to deliver the gospel message? God tells us through the apostle Paul in the book of Romans, *How then will they call on him in whom they have not believed? And how are they to believe in him of whom they have never heard? And how are they to hear without someone preaching? And how are they to preach unless they are sent? As it is written, "How beautiful are the feet of those who preach the good news!"* (Romans 10:14–15, ESV).

If you follow these six guideposts, you will be more effective in sharing your faith with others. Now that we have a plan for sharing our faith using apologetics in evangelism, let's look at one of the most important elements that undergird our ability to reach others—empathy.

APPLYING EMPATHY TO EVANGELISM

Take a few moments to remember when you did not know God or have a relationship with Jesus Christ. Ponder what that was like and how different your life was then as compared to now. In all honesty, you were then lost, but now you have been found by God (Luke 15:24; John

9:25). It is easy for us as Christians to take for granted the empathy God extended to you and me. In his love, Jesus Christ died for us when we were still his enemies: *But God demonstrates his own love for us in this: While we were still sinners, Christ died for us* (Romans 5:8). It's convenient for us as Christians to be complacent and withhold empathy from others when sharing our faith. It is much easier for us to judge others' religious beliefs than muster the courage to share our faith with them. Making the effort to share our faith with others entails time, energy, courage, and an empathetic heart. It is more comfortable for us to live within the safety of the Christian community than to step out into the cruel world and share our faith. It is right for us to enter into Christian community, but we cannot lock the door behind us.

If we live in the Christian bubble full time, we risk becoming Club-Christians. Club Christians act more like museum curators for the saved than hospital doctors for the unsaved. Not that churches should solely cater to the unsaved, but they should be actively reaching the unsaved. You can avoid becoming part of the Christian bubble by remembering where you came from and appreciating the empathy and grace the Lord extended to you when you were lost. Empathy is a vital companion of apologetics in evangelism because it becomes an extension of God's love and yours.

We are commanded to speak *the truth in love* (Ephesians 4:15), not the truth *or* love. When we show empathy toward those who are not Christians, we crack open the door to that person's heart, often giving them the freedom to share the secret places in their personal life, their religious beliefs, and the obstacles that may be impeding their belief in the Christian faith. Extending empathy toward others will also enable you to better understand your audience, and understanding your audience is essential to sharing your faith with them.

KNOWING YOUR AUDIENCE

Knowing whom you are speaking with will help you to tailor the gospel message in a way that resonates with that individual or group of people. Knowing your audience will, in turn, earn the respect of your listeners. Earning their respect will, by default, attract their attention. At this point, you have earned the right to be heard. This is not only true of others but also of you and me. For example, my good friend Michael Keating knew I loved to play racquetball. He kept inviting me to go to his Bible study and then play racquetball. I kept declining until he invited me to play racquetball and then go to his Bible study. The racquetball motivated me to agree to attend the Bible study. Once there, I committed to that Bible study and was invited to join a small-group Bible study with four mature Christians. Making the effort to know your audience is essential.

Whether you are speaking to an individual or a group of people, you can do a number of things in advance to ensure that you gain their interest and the right to be heard. First, make sure you understand the point you are trying to make and be able to support your message with Scripture and apologetics as needed.

Second, don't assume the person(s) to whom you are speaking is like you. He or she may have cultural, geographic, religious, or even emotional biases contrary to your own. People who do not share my Christian worldview are often open to talking about God, the meaning of life, and eternity. In most cases, they are less interested in arguing or debating than in discovering the truth about God. If we don't make the effort to know whom we are speaking with, we will never earn the right to talk more deeply with them in the first place.

Third, know, as best as you can, the person or group's cultural beliefs, worldview, level of Bible knowledge, and knowledge of theology. Sharing the basic truths of the Christian faith in a major city should be different than sharing the same message in a rural town. One is not better than the other. They are different people groups with different cultures, and we need to see each demographic as different culturally but still one race—the human race created in God's image.

Lastly, be aware of how you dress, your body language and hand gestures, choice of humor, and how yo u communicate in relation to your audience.[4] Trust me, having been born in Brooklyn, NY, raised in Washington, DC, and having lived in North Carolina for over twenty years, I have learned the hard way that it is wise to know your audience. For example, speaking to *you guys* (or *yuse guys*) in New York City is different than speaking to *y'all* in rural North Carolina.

In addition to knowing your audience, remember that when you share your faith with non-Christians, you are sharing your faith with those of the natural world. The natural person is not committed to Jesus Christ or Christianity; he or she is *in* and *of* the natural world. Just like you and I were years ago. Being an effective Christian witness and sharing your supernatural faith in a natural world is as much of an art as it is a science.

SHARING YOUR FAITH IN THE NATURAL WORLD

We can't expect those that we share the truth of God with to be on the same page as us spiritually because they do not have a Christian worldview, do not have the Holy Spirit living in their hearts, and are not depending on or trusting in Jesus Christ as Lord and Savior. By their very nature, they are unable to accept the gospel message in full at that point in their life. The Bible tells us, *The natural person does not accept the things of the Spirit of God, for they are folly to him, and he is not able to understand them because they are spiritually discerned* (1 Corinthians 2:14, ESV). Sharing your faith in the natural world needs the use of apologetics in tandem with evangelism. Apologetics not only removes obstacles but also shows others that we can answer difficult questions through extra-biblical evidence that supports and validates the Bible. As a result, we Christians can avoid being mis-categorized as ignorant, uneducated, and ill informed. In reality, Christians are some of the most educated and informed people in the world. Some non-believers attempt to make Christians look bad to make the Bible and Christianity look foolish or false. Being equipped with apologetics in addition to the Bible will help you to avoid this.

Looking back to the story at the opening of this chapter, I learned a couple of good lessons. The first lesson is that by being equipped with apologetics for evangelism, we are better equipped to give answers for the Christian faith than some of the smartest (non-believing) people in the natural world. The second lesson is that when we share our faith in the natural world, there are usually more people watching and hearing our presentation of the gospel and the Christian message than we are aware of.

THE FRUITS OF CONVERSATIONAL EVANGELISM IN WASHINGTON, DC

When I worked at the computer software company in Washington, DC, one of my coworkers was a young lady from Barbados. As the receptionist at our office, she diligently and faithfully executed her job, answering the phones with a servant's heart. Without a fancy title or management position, she served others and never got involved in theological conversations. Nobody in the company, including me, knew much if anything about her worldview or religious background.

At that time, I was helping a friend at church get counseling. I used the money from my small side business to pay for my friend's counseling sessions. Because of this arrangement, I had to schedule each week's counseling session, which required the assistance of the receptionist. Week in and week out, she helped me to facilitate phone calls, unknown to the rest of the office. I didn't have a direct dial to my desk, so when calls came in on the general line, she confidentially alerted me to callbacks from the counselor's office. In a broad sense, without breaching confidentiality, I shared the situation with her in relation to what I was doing, and she was very kind to help me.

About a week after I retired from that company, the receptionist called me at my home. She said, "Steve, I want to thank you so much for everything you've done for me and my husband." Perplexed, I asked her what I had done for her and her husband, considering I had never met her husband. She replied, "Through watching how you lived out the Christian faith, your love for God and for other people, I felt compelled to re-examine my own life and marriage. By watching how you defended the truth of

God while still loving others, I was convicted in my own faith."

She went on to tell me that when she and her husband lived in Barbados, they were very committed to their church and had a strong walk with Christ. When they relocated to the United States, however, they walked away from the church and their faith to a great extent. She went on to tell me, "My husband and I have now found and committed ourselves to a great church right here in the DC area. As a result, we've both recommitted our lives to Jesus Christ and are once again growing in the Lord and in our marriage. Thank you, Steve."

God has a funny way of using us when we least expect it. This young lady and her husband were impacted by my willingness to help a friend with counseling, the conversations I had with the antagonistic computer scientist, my friend from Turkey, and others through the numerous conversations we had in the main conference room during our daily lunch breaks. After I hung up the phone with her and thought about our conversation, I evaluated what I had done well and what I might have done better. Was I too bold? Was I too timid? Was I offensive? Did I argue, or did I reason for truth from the Scriptures? I concluded I was able to utilize apologetics in sharing my faith through conversational evangelism. I was careful not to run around the office hitting people with the Bible, but I also didn't shirk from either standing on what the Bible says in relation to the contemporary issues or the deity of Jesus Christ. God had simply chosen to use me. He worked through my imperfections to achieve His will as a result of my obedience to Him in stepping out in faith to share Christ with others. That, along with being equipped by studying my Bible and using some basic apologetics, is what I did right, and by God's grace, His will was done.

My experience was similar to what the apostle Paul did in reasoning for truth as he used the Scriptures, philosophy, logic, and theology—*speaking the truth in love* (Ephesians 4:15). You and I can become all things to all people and relate to different people in different ways to win some to Jesus Christ. Paul put it this way:

> *For though I am free from all, I have made myself a servant to all that I might win more of them. To the Jews I became as a Jew, in order to win Jews. To those under the law I became as one under the law (though not being myself under the law) that I might win those under the law. To those outside the law I became as one outside the law (not being outside the law of God but under the law of Christ) that I might win those outside the law. To the weak I became weak, that I might win the weak. I have become all things to all people that by all means I might save some. I do it all for the sake of the gospel, that I may share with them in its blessings.* (1 Corinthians 9:19–23, ESV)

In the case of the job in Washington, DC, to the computer scientist I became an intellectual, to the receptionist I became a compassionate servant and communicator, to my friend from Turkey I became an open-minded philosopher—so I might win some for Jesus Christ. I don't always get it all right, but by God's grace, I was able to share the truth of God with those who held worldviews very different from my own. I didn't shirk from difficult discussions about the existence of God, moral issues, or the origin of mankind (creation vs. evolution). I applied apologetics, even though I hadn't yet heard the word *apologetics*. I was roughly trained with extra-biblical evidence and some basic scientific studies about specific issues by my pastor Lon Solomon, from listening to the *Focus on the Family* and *Family Life Today* radio stations, along with other Christian resources. As a result, I became equipped to defend and advance the truth of God.

Whether evangelizing, reasoning from truth and logic using apologetics, or simply having a discussion with your coworkers about the Bible, look to the apostle Paul as a role model for giving reasons for truth and allow the Holy Spirit to change the hearts of those with whom you share the gospel. We are the messengers, not the message. By simultaneously reasoning with the mind and appealing to the heart, God will use you and me in great ways to win some to Jesus Christ, if we are willing—and equipped.

Conclusion

And he gave the apostles, the prophets, the evangelists, the shepherds and teachers, to equip the saints for the work of ministry. (Ephesians 4:11–12, ESV)

Looking back at the three mountain climbers who perished attempting to climb 11,239-foot Mt. Hood in Oregon, it seems obvious that they were not equipped for the unforeseen challenges that lay ahead of them. Although all three men were experienced climbers, they all perished. All of them also possessed the very best gear. But having the best gear and a lot of experience did not mean that they were equipped for the unforeseen challenges they faced on that tragic trip.

As of 2007, about 10,000 people attempted to climb Mount Hood each year.[1] One of the worst climbing accidents occurred in 1986 when seven teenagers and two schoolteachers froze to death while attempting to retreat from a storm.[2] No matter what route is chosen, Mount Hood is a technical climb. Ropes, crampons (spikes attached to climbing boots), and ice axes are required to ascend and descend the mountain.

Not every climbing accident is caused by a failure to be equipped; accidents and unforeseen circumstances beyond our control do arise. This is the reality of life. Despite the ill-fated climbers' available gear and years of experience, they packed light in order to ascend and descend quickly. But they were not equipped with the proper gear or supplies to survive an unforeseen storm. Furthermore, none of them brought an emergency GPS that could send out a signal via satellite so rescuers could pinpoint the climbers' location and retrieve them. One of the climbers made a snow cave, and for a short time was able to converse with his wife on the phone. But that was not enough information to confirm his location and to find him before he froze to death.

The failure to be equipped comes with consequences, here on earth and in eternity.

Approximately 70 percent of Christian teens who attend college walk away from their faith, most by the end of their freshman year.[3] Upon entering the secular college campus, many of these students believe they are equipped to defend their faith in an environment hostile to the existence of God and to Christianity.

Most other Christians also believe they are equipped to defend their faith. In our workplaces, neighborhoods, family gatherings, and, sadly enough, in some of our churches, all too often students and non-student alike know what they believe but not why they believe what they believe. It is a gamble of epic proportion for students, parents, and grandparents.

Many Christians over the age of sixty are also leaving the church because they see the encroaching culture of change and the digital age as dumbing down the Christian faith. Correct in so many cases, they perceive modern preaching as more focused on self-help than on biblical truth. They believe the church has lost its way.[4] Unfortunately, the loss of the older generation creates a greater problem in that their absence depletes churches of one of their most precious resources—wise, experienced, and seasoned Christians who can disciple younger generations.

According to Dr. Mark Gray, a senior research associate at the Center for Applied Research in the Apostolate at Georgetown University, "young Catholics are leaving the faith … sometimes before the age of ten … saying they are atheist or agnostic. …They are bringing up things that are related to science and a need for evidence and a need for proof." In other words, they lack training in apologetics. "It's almost a crisis of faith," Dr. Gray said. "In the whole concept of faith, this is a generation that is struggling with faith in ways that we haven't seen in previous generations."[5] The lack of being equipped from youth to retirement is prompting an entire generation of Christians to doubt, deny, and walk away from their faith. This is not *almost* a crisis of faith—it *is* a crisis of faith.

Thankfully, God has provided a solution—apologetics. We can appeal to the heart and equip the mind to reason from the Scriptures. Apologetics equips Christians so they can show how science, logic, and a vast body of evidence support the Christian faith.

Climbing Mt. Hood, or any mountain for that matter, is like living the Christian faith. For starters, we should be looking up, always focused on the peak. As we seek God and maintain a relationship with him, we will always have logical questions. Many of those questions can be answered or supported with apologetics. But in the end, having faith in God is the most crucial part of our life journey. The Bible should always be the main authority and the primary source of our training and equipping.

Apologetics is a tool in the toolbox that will help us by way of understanding theology, systematic Bible study, science, logic, and extra-biblical evidence. Being equipped with apologetics for evangelism means three things. First, it means being equipped with apologetics in general. We have covered some of the most basic questions that all Christians and most non-Christians ask in evaluating their faith in God or lack thereof. We first established that everyone has a worldview, and we helped readers better define their own worldview as a start point. We laid out evidence for the existence of God and then showed why all world religions and gods cannot lead to one central God.

In other words, all roads don't lead to heaven or to the same God. Second, we laid out how we know that we are going to heaven and how to commit our lives to God and receive eternal life through Jesus Christ. We discussed why God allows evil to exist in the first place and how we can understand and share with others why God allows bad things, such as pain and suffering, to happen to good people. Third, we addressed how to better defend our truth in a culture hostile to the Christian faith as well as how to advance our faith using apologetics in evangelism.

Every day we live on this earth represents another opportunity to give an answer (a defense) for the hope that lies within us. Using apologetics in evangelism, as well as speaking truth and demonstrating love, represents an opportunity to share our faith with a dying world. We live in a multicultural world and country, so we must understand other cultures, their people, their religious beliefs, and their worldviews if we are to reach them personally. We must be equipped to defend and advance the Christian faith in the twenty-first century, or we will miss both the opportunities the Lord brings our way to provide answers about the Christian faith and the privilege to show others the truth of the Christian faith.

Ascending the mountain can be compared to evangelizing, descending the mountain to defending your faith after reaching the peak. Descending is often more dangerous than ascending because supplies are depleted and the body is exhausted. One also has to defend against unforeseen dangers that can develop during this segment of the trip. If we are not equipped, we will miss the opportunities to lead others to the summit (peak). If we are not equipped, we—along with our children and many young people, including students—will get fatigued and walk away from the Christian faith even after we reach the summit of commitment to Christ. We live in a different world than our parents and grandparents did. We live in a world where apologetics and apologetics in evangelism are essential to our lives, to our personal God-given mission, and the advancement of our faith.

In generations past, the Bible and the message of salvation found in Jesus Christ were all we needed to share our faith because most people agreed, even if they were not committed Christians, that the Bible was the truth, even if they did not pursue it as such. In today's progressive, postmodern, global society, we encounter multiculturalism and religious views very different from the Christian faith. Telling our kids to just hang in there does not work because it leaves them vulnerable to the cultural pressure and societal norms generated by other belief systems. Neither can we leave our faith in a dormant, idle stage. The only constant is change, and if we are not continually learning to be equipped, we may lose out on many opportunities where God might have used us.

If we understand our own worldview, we can help others see that they not only have a worldview but also what that worldview is. Many Christians who attend church do not have a Christian worldview, so how can they accurately convey it to others? Next, we need to be able to show that the evidence found in science and archeology prove that Christianity is true—not the opposite.

Once we better understand the evidence for God's existence, we can converse intelligently with atheists and agnostics. We can also help ourselves, our children, neighbors, coworkers, and others who doubt God's existence come to accept his existence. This is essential to pre-evangelism.

Once we establish that God exists, we have to be able to show that there is only one true God and that none of the other gods and religions can lead to heaven. One of the ways we do that is through providing evidence of the resurrection of Jesus Christ. Every worldview and religion has its own idea of what and who God is. The difference between Christianity and all other belief systems is that all the other gods die, and they are never resurrected. Jesus died, was buried, and three days later rose from the dead—exactly how the Old Testament Scriptures prophesied and in accordance with what Jesus himself proclaimed prior to his death and resurrection. Jesus is unique among all other gods and religions because he is the truth.

Once we establish that Jesus supernaturally rose from the dead we will need to answer one of the most common objections to Christianity: what evil is and why an all-powerful, just, and loving God would allow evil in the form of pain, suffering, and loss. One of the best ways to share your faith using apologetics is to help others see that God is unable to sin or do evil.

This leads us to address moral issues, another gateway for us to share our faith. Most every issue covered in the media has at its root a moral dilemma—from crooked politicians to the #METOO movement to welfare to corporate greed to sexual norms. People want to know that there is an ultimate moral standard in our chaotic world. All cultures at all times agree that murder, rape, and theft are wrong. By establishing that there are moral absolutes, we can make the case for an Absolute Moral Maker—God. Once we do all those things, we can lay out exactly how someone knows he or she is going to heaven and how to trust in Jesus Christ as the only way to heaven.

BEING *EQUIPPED* IS NOT OPTIONAL

It's time that we as the church reverse the trend of an entire generation abandoning their faith. Had those Mt. Hood climbers been equipped with a simple device known as a GPS beacon, they most likely would be alive today. If we are equipped with apologetics for evangelism, we will keep our faith alive and help others and ourselves thrive in the Christian faith. But, if we are able but not willing to step out and share our faith, we will miss the blessing of God working through us to fulfill the Great Commission (Matthew 28:16–20). If we are willing but ill equipped to evangelize in the natural (secular) world of the new age, we will be ineffective and, in most cases, miss out on the opportunities God brings us to defend Christianity and share the truth of God with others. Sometimes this means sharing more from your heart; other times, it means sharing more from your mind. It means having courage as well as the willingness and ability to answer the tough questions about God, eternity, and salvation (Romans 10:14–15).

Like the apostle Paul who removed obstacles during his presentation of the gospel at Iconium—where he proclaimed the gospel on his first, second, and third missionary journeys—we too must be equipped to present the gospel. We must speak so effectively the *oracles of God* (1 Peter 4:11) that those with whom we share the gospel will want to accept God's gift of salvation and entrust their life here on earth and in eternity to Jesus Christ.

By being equipped to use apologetics in evangelism, you will be able to better help lost individuals move closer to God. You will help some move from a place of disbelief in God or a place of vague interest in spirituality to a more specific interest in the claims of Jesus Christ and Christianity. Sometimes, you will also have the privilege to be used by God to lead others to new life in Jesus Christ. This is the eternal importance of being equipped!

To see a list of additional resources, to request that Steven speak at your church, organization, or group, and to find other books written by Steven, please proceed to page 167: *Additional Resources and Contact Information*.

ADDITIONAL RESOURCES

Blog: **reasonfortruth.org/home/rft-blog**
Podcast: **reasonfortruth.org/podcast-video**
Books/Resources: **reasonfortruth.org/resources**
Seminars: **reasonfortruth.org/equippedseminars**

CONTACT STEVEN

Steven speaks frequently on the topic of *Theology, Apologetics, and Using Apologetics in Evangelism.* He can deliver a keynote, partial day, half-day, or full-day version of this content, depending on your needs. If you are interested in finding out more, please contact Steven at *reasonfortruth.org/equippedseminars/host-a-seminar.*

To submit a request for Steven to speak at an event:
reasonfortruth.org/equippedseminars/request-speaker

You can also connect with Steven on social media:
Facebook: **facebook.com/ReasonForTruth.org**
Twitter: **twitter.com/steve_garofalo**
Web Site: **ReasonForTruth.Org**
(ReasonForTruth.Bible)

Endnotes

INTRODUCTION

1. Roy B. Zuck, *The Speakers Quote Book, Over 4,500 Illustrations and Quotations for all Occasions*, (Grand Rapids, MI: Kregel Publications, 1997) 312.

2. William Yardley, "Searchers Scale Back Search for 2 Climbers on Mount Hood," *The New York Times*, December 20, 2006, http://www.nytimes.com/2006/12/20/us/20climbers.html

3. Cathy Lynn Grossman, "Young Adults Aren't Sticking With Church," *USA Today*, March 19, 2011, 6D. https://usatoday30.usatoday.com/printedition/life/20070807/d_churchdropout07.art.htm

4. "Youth Exodus Problem," CrossExamined.org, 2014, https://crossexamined.org/youth-exodus-problem/

5. Noelle Crombie, "Three Stranded on Mt. Hood Identified," *The Oregonian*. December 11, 2006. http://blog.oregonlive.com/clackamascounty/2008/11/two_earli-

er_rescue_attempts_tw.html

6. Merriam-Webster's definition of "prove": http://www.merriam-webster.com/dictionary/.prove

7. Chris Mitchell, *Praying for Joy…Behar*, CBN News, February 18, 2018, https://www1.cbn.com/cbnnews/us/2018/february/praying-for-joy-hellip-behar-nbsp

CHAPTER 1

Everyone As A Worldview: What's Yours?

1. James Anderson, *What Is a Worldview?* Ligonier Blog, June 21, 2017, Ligonier Ministries the teaching fellowship of R.C. Sproul, https://www.ligonier.org/blog/what-worldview/

2. Steven Garofalo, *Right for You, but Not for Me—A Response to Moral Relativism*, (Charlotte, N.C.: Triedstone Publishing Company, 2013), 253.

3. Garofalo, *Right for You*, 202.

4. Winfried Corduan, *A Christian Introduction to World Religions Neighboring Faiths*, Downers Grove, Ill.: InterVarsity Press, 1998), 189.

5. Norman L. Geisler, *I Don't Have Enough Faith to Be an Atheist*, (Wheaton, Ill: Crossway Books, 2004), 57.

6. *What Is a Worldview?* The American Scientific Affiliation, http://asa3.org/ASA/education/views/index.html.

7. Norman L. Geisler, *Baker Encyclopedia of Christian Apologetics*, (Grand Rapids, Mich.: Baker Books, 2000), 786-787.

8. A.W. Tozer, *The Knowledge of the Holy*, (New York, N.Y.: HarperSanFrancisco, 1961), 1.

9. Geisler, *Baker Encyclopedia*, 786.

10. Charles C. Ryrie, *Basic Theology* (Chicago: Moody Press, 1999), 46.

11. Norman Geisler, *Systematic Theology In One Volume* (Minneapolis, Minnesota: Bethany House, 2011), 17, 31.

12. Wayne A. Detzer and Douglas E. Potter, *Cross Cultural Apologetics—Bridging Culture to Defend the Faith*, 2011 Wayne A. Detzer and Douglas E. Potter, 129–132.

13. Geisler, *Baker Encyclopedia of Christian Apologetics*, (Grand Rapids, Mich.: Baker Books, 2000), 724.

14. Geisler, *Baker Encyclopedia*, 337.

15. Geisler, *Baker Encyclopedia*,722–23.

16. Geisler, *Baker Encyclopedia*, 786.

17. Geisler, *Baker Encyclopedia*, 786.

18. Geisler, *Baker Encyclopedia*, 786.

19. Geisler, *Baker Encyclopedia*, 786.

CHAPTER 2
Does God Exist?

1. Edward Young, *Night Thoughts*. Night v, 1.177

2. Norman L. Geisler, *Baker Encyclopedia of Christian Apologetics*, (Grand Rapids, Mich.: Baker Books, 2000), 174.

3. Geisler, *Baker Encyclopedia*, 214.

4. Geisler, *Baker Encyclopedia*, 711.

5. Nick Herbert, *Quantum Reality—Beyond the New Physics, and The Meaning of Reality*, (New York, NY: Anchor Books A Division of Random House, Inc., 1987), 176.

6. Lynde Landgon, "Einstein's academic heirs win physics Nobel," The Sift-World Magazine, (October 3, 2017), https://world.wng.org/content/einstein_s_academic_heirs_win_physics_nobel.

7. Entropy Law, *All About Entropy, The Laws Of Thermodynamics, And Order From Disorder*, Copyright 2001 Archives of Science www.entropylaw.com

8. Ibid.

9. Norman L. Geisler and Frank Turek, *Why I Have Enough Faith To Be An Atheist* (Wheaton, IL: Crossway Books, 2004), 75.

10. Geisler and Turek, 78-79.

11. Geisler, *Baker Encyclopedia*, 174.

12. Geisler and Turek, 95.

13. Geisler, *Baker Encyclopedia*, 574

14. Geisler, *Baker Encyclopedia*, 574.

15. Paley, Evidences 10, 11, 16, 17, 20, 29.

16. Mario Seiglie, *DNA: The Tiny Code That's Toppling Evolution*, The Good News Magazine (May-June 2005), at http://www/ucg.org/science/dna-tiny-code-thats-toppling-evolution/.

17. Jessilyn Justice, *Genetics Experts Confirms the Reality of Adam and Eve*, CharismaN-ews, 2:00PM EDT 7/28/2015 http://www.charismanews.com/world/50749-ge-netics-expert-confirms-the-reality-of-adam-and-eve

18. Nathaniel T. Jeanson, Ph.D., *New Genetic-Clock Research Challenges Millions of Years*, Evidence for Creation, Institute Creation Research, http://www.icr.org/arti-cle/8017/

19. Tia Ghose, Staff Writer, "Genetic 'Adam' and 'Eve' Uncovered," LiveScience.Com August 1, 2013 02:000pm ET http://www.livescience.com/38613-genetic-ad-am-and-eve-uncovered.html

20. Ghose.

21. Justice.

22. Geisler, *Baker Encyclopedia*, 26.

23. Charles Ryrie, *The Ryrie Study Bible, New International Version*, Chicago, IL, 1984), 1545.

24. Ryrie, 1543.

25. Geisler, *Baker Encyclopedia*, 174.

26. Robert Jastrow, *God and the Astronomers* (New York: Norton, 1978), 116.

CHAPTER 3

COEXIST: Do All Religious Roads Lead to Heaven?

1. Miguel de Unamuno—*The Tragic Sense of Life*, 8.

2. Norman L. Geisler, *Baker Encyclopedia of Christian Apologetics*, (Grand Rapids, Mich.: Baker Books, 2000), 598

3. Geisler, *BECA*, 598.

4. Geisler, *Pluralism*, PowerPoint classroom presentation, copyright, 2005, Slide 6.

5. Debra Lardie, *Concise Dictionary of the Occult and New Age*, (Grand Rapids, MI: Kregel Publications, 2000), 183.

6. Yutaka J. Amano and Norman L. Geisler, *The Infiltration of the New Age*, (Wheaton, Ill.: Tyndale House Publishers, Inc., 1989), 18.

7. Ron Rhodes, *The Challenge of the Cults and New Religions*, (Grand Rapids, Mich.: Zondervan, 2001), 129.

8. Marilyn Ferguson, review of *Heaven on Earth* by Michael D'Antonio, Los Angeles Times, 16, February 1993.

9. *New Age Spirituality: Part 1 of 2, a.k.a. Self-spirituality, New spirituality, Mind-body-spirit*, Ontario Consultants on Religious Tolerance. Latest update: April 13th 2015, http://www.religioustolerance.org/newage.htm.

10. George Barna, "The Index of Leading Spiritual Indicators," Word Publishing, Dallas TX, (1996)

11. David Spangler, *Reflections of the Christ*, (Findhorn, Scotland: Findhorn, 1978), 40.

12. Amano and Geisler, *Infiltration*, 116.

13. Amano and Geisler, *Infiltration*, 125.

14. Ron Rhodes, *The Counterfeit Christ of The New Age Movement*, (Grand Rapids: Baker Book House, 1990), 168.

15. Ron Rhodes, *The Counterfeit Christ of The New Age Movement*, (Grand Rapids: Baker Book House, 1990), 168.

16. Geisler, *Baker Encyclopedia*, 250.

17. Geisler, *Pluralism*, slide 40.

18. Lardie, *Concise Dictionary*, 130.

19. Geisler, *Pluralism*, Slide 6.

20. Norman Geisler, *Pluralism*, Slide 6.

CHAPTER 4

Did Jesus Really Rise from the Dead?

1. William Lane Craig, "Did Jesus Rise from the Dead?", in *Jesus Under Fire: Modern Scholarship Reinvents the Historical Jesus*, eds. Michael J. Wilkins and J.P. Moreland (Grand Rapids, MI: Zondervan Publishing House, 1995), 141-176.

2. Norman Geisler, "Historiography: The Historical Precondition", in *Systematic Theology*, Vol. 1(Minneapolis, MN: Bethany House, 2002), 181-204. [emphasis in original]

3. Geisler, 181-204.

4. Geisler, 181-204.

5. Craig L. Blomberg, "The Historical Reliability of the New Testament," in William Lane Craig's *Reasonable Faith, 2nd ed.* (Wheaton, IL: Crossway Books, 1994), 193-231.

6. Gary Habermas, "Did Jesus Perform Miracles?", in *Jesus Under Fire: Modern Scholarship Reinvents the Historical Jesus*, eds. Michael J. Wilkins and J.P. Moreland (Grand Rapids, MI: Zondervan Publishing House, 1995), 118-140.

7. F.F. Bruce, *The New Testament Documents: Are They Reliable?*, (Grand Rapids, MI: Inter-Varsity Press, 1998), 16-17.

8. Bruce Metzger, *The Text of the New Testament: Its Transmission, Corruption, and Restoration, 3rd ed.* (Oxford, Oxford University Press, 1992), 33-35.

9. Metzger, 36.

10. Bruce,19.

11. As an aside, it is clarifying to note the difference between the history of the New Testament documents and the history of the Islamic Qu'ran. In the history of the Qu'ran. there were times where copies of the book that had what we would call today "textual variants" were collected and burned. This significantly shaped the genealogies of the manuscripts so that the possibility of getting back to the original from one's current copies becomes less likely. In contrast, the New Testament documents not similarly treated so that they retain textual variants that are 'pure', that is, show a distinct genealogical pathway that helps scholars trace a reading back to the original.

12. Gary Habermas, *The Risen Jesus & Future Hope*, (New York: Roman & Littlefield Publishers, 2003), 9.

13. N.T. Wright, "Appendix B" in Antony Flew's T*here is a God: How the World's Most Notorious Atheist Changed His Mind* (New York: Harper One, 2008), 185-213.

14. Wright, 185-213.

CHAPTER 5

Why Does God Allow Bad Things to Happen to Good People?

1. Billy Graham, *Till Armageddon*, (Waco, TX: Word, 1981), 51.

2. Ann O'Neil, "The Reinvention of Ted Turner" CNN, (November 17, 2013 10:30 AM EST.) at http://www.cnn.com/2013/11/17/us/ted-turner-profile/index.html.

3. Wayne Jackson, "Meet Ted Turner-Thanks, I'd Rather Not!" Christian Courier, (February 7, 2018), at https://www.christiancourier.com/articles/1-meet-ted-turner-thanks-id-rather-not

4. Norman L. Geisler, ***Baker Encyclopedia of Christian Apologetics***. (Grand Rapids: Baker Books, 2000), 220.

5. Geisler, *Baker Encyclopedia*, 220.

6. Geisler, *Baker Encyclopedia*, 220.

7. Geisler, *Baker Encyclopedia*, 220.

8. Dinesh D'Souza "Why We Need Earthquakes," *Muddling Toward Maturity Blog.. embracing the true, discarding the false*, (Monday, 04 May 2009), at http://muddling-towardmaturity.typepad.com/my_weblog/2009/05/dinesh-dsouza-why-we-need-earthquakes.html.

9. Natasha Crain, *Keeping Your Kids on God's Side, 40 Conversations to Help Them Build a Lasting Faith*, (Eugene, Oregon: Harvest House Publishers, 2016), 26.

10. Dinesh D'Douza, "Why We Need Earthquakes," *Christianity Today*, (April 28, 2009), at http://www.christianitytoday.com/ct/2009/may/12:58.html?start=1.

11. Norman L. Geisler, *If God, Why Evil*? PowerPoint presentation Derived from *Baker Encyclopedia*.

12. Geisler, *If God*.

13. Geisler, *If God*.

14. Geisler, *If God*.

CHAPTER 6

How Do I Explain Evil, Pain, and Suffering to Others?

1. Billy Graham, *The Journey,* (Nashville: W Publishing Group, 2006), 197.

2. Norman L. Geisler, *Baker Encyclopedia of Christian Apologetics*, (Grand Rapids, MI: Baker Books, 2000), 222.

3. C. S. Lewis, *Mere Christianity*, (New York, NY: HarperCollins Publishers, 1952), 48.

4. Norman L. Geisler, *If God, Why Evil?*, PowerPoint presentation. Derived from BECA.

5. Norman L. Geisler, *Systematic Theology In One Volume*, (Minneapolis, Minnesota: Bethany House, 2011), 795.

6. Billy Graham, *Till Armageddon*, (Waco, TX: Word, 1981), 191.

CHAPTER 7

Is Morality Relative?

1. *Aine Cain, A day in the life of a Playboy bunny, and how the controversial job has changed over 60 years*, Business Insider, 4:30PM 9/28/2017 http://www.businessinsider.com/playboy-bunnies-history-2017-9/#the-name-comes-from-an-unexpected-source-as-a-university-of-illinois-student-hefner-would-sometimes-dine-at-bunnys-tavern-in-urbana-illinois-apparently-the-name-stuck-with-him-1

2. Quoted in Katrina Trinko, *The Human Costs of the World Hugh Hefner Created*, The Daily Signal, 9/28/2017 http://dailysignal.com//print?post_id=359466

3. Trinko, Human Costs.

4. Norman L. Geisler, *Baker Encyclopedia of Christian Apologetics*, (Grand Rapids, MI: Baker Books, 2000), 501.

5. Trinko, *Human Costs.*

6. Keith Crim, General Editor, *The Perennial Dictionary Of World Religions* (New York: Harper Collins Publishers, 1989), 677.

7. *Teen People*, August 2003, "Brad Pitt answering a question about what defines the teenage years," 112.

8. Alan Bloom, *The Closing of the American Mind* (New York: Simon and Schuster, 1987), 25.

9. Trinko, *Human Costs*.

10. Hollie McKay, *Exclusive: High Hefner Wants the 'Love of His Life' Holly Madison to Return to Mansion*, FoxNews.Com, Tuesday, 4/28/2009 http://www.foxnews.com/story/0,2933,518219,00.html

CHAPTER 8

How Do I Know That I Am Going to Heaven?

1. Billy Graham, *The Journey* (Nashville: W Publishing Group, 2006), 73.

2. *Steps to Peace with God* witnessing tract, Crossway.org, published 2006, Good News Publishers and Crossway Books. Public Domain. Used with permission of the Billy Graham Evangelistic Association.

CHAPTER 9

How Do I Use Apologetics to Defend the Christian Faith?

1. "Apologetics," Merriam-Webster Dictionary, https://www.merriam-webster.com/dictionary/apologetics

2. Ron Rhodes, *5–Minute Apologetics for Today*, (Eugene, OR: Harvest House Publishers), Copyright 2010 Ron Rhodes.

3. Norman L. Geisler, *Christian Apologetics*, Second Edition, (Grand Rapids, MI: Baker Academic), Copyright 2013 Norman L. Geisler, x.

4. Norman L. Geisler and Frank Turek, *I Don't Have Enough Faith to Be an Atheist*, (Wheaton, Ill.: Crossway Books), Copyright 2004, Norman L. Geisler and Frank Turek.

5. Geisler and Turek, *I Don't Have Enough Faith*, 40.

CHAPTER 10
HOW CAN I USE APOLOGETICS IN CONVERSATIONAL PRE-EVANGELISM?

1. Billy Graham, *Just As I Am* (San Francisco: HarperOne, 1997), 696.

2. CBN News, *Three Things Christians Should Pray for Ahead of Billy Graham's Funeral*, John Jessup, February 23, 2018, http://www1.cbn.com/cbnnews/2018/february/three-things-christians-should-pray-for-ahead-of-billy-graham-rsquo-s-funeral

3. Ray Ciervo, *Apologetics for The Rest of Us: A Beginners Guide*, (Maitland, FL: Xulon Press, 2013), 25–26.

4. ASME, *Public Speaking: Know Your Audience*, Tom Ricci, August 2012, https://www.asme.org/career-education/articles/public-speaking/public-speaking-know-your-audience

CONCLUSION

1. Aimee Green, Mark Larabee and Katy Muldoon (February 19, 2007). "Everything goes right in Mount Hood Search," The Oregonian/OregonLive.com. Retrieved 2007-09-21.

2. Last Body Recovered from Mount Hood," CBS. May 31, 2002. Retrieved 2007-05-25.

3. Michael F. Haverluck, *Ministries tackle 70% rate of college students leaving faith*, One News Now, Sunday, August 13, 2017. https://www.onenewsnow.com/church/2017/08/13/ministries-tackle-70-rate-of-college-students-leaving-faith

4. Joe LaGuardia, *3 Reasons People Over 60 Leave Your Church*, Ethics Daily, Septem-

ber 22, 2015, https://www.ethicsdaily.com/3-reasons-people-over-60-leave-your-church-cms-22952/

5. Matt Hadro, *Why Catholics are leaving the faith by age 10–and what parents can do about it*, CRUX, December 18, 2016, https://cruxnow.com/cna/2016/12/18/catholics-leaving-faith-age-10-parents-can/